Tessa Kiros

LIMONCELLO
And
LINEN WATER

Tessa Kiros

LIMONCELLO
And
LINEN WATER

A Trousseau of Italian Recipes

PHOTOGRAPHY
MANOS CHATZIKONSTANTIS

STYLING
MICHAIL TOUROS

ART DIRECTION
LISA GREENBERG

MURDOCH BOOKS

TO ALL OF THE
WONDERFUL MATRIARCHS I HAVE
BEEN LUCKY TO MEET.

For Yasmine & Cassia
For Wilma who gives with both hands

CONTENTS

INTRODUCTION

- viii -

THE LINEN CUPBOARD

- 1 -

THE PANTRY

- 10 -

THE BREAD OVEN

- 46 -

THE SNACK BOX

- 70 -

THE VEGETABLE PATCH

- 88 -

THE PASTA POT

- 118 -

THE DINING ROOM

- 160 -

THE SUGAR BIN

- 262 -

THE ICE BOX

- 302 -

Introduction

This book is inspired by my mother-in-law Wilma and the many other wonder women that roam freely about. Wilma is a shining beacon of inspiration — never missing a step while busily folding, soaking, plopping and puffing things out of thin air. She always has the right colour button or shade of Italian cotton handy and a pair of scissors tied and tucked into the inside pocket of her handbag. She is chock-a-block full of herbs and recipes, energy and ideas, love and inspiration. She has knowledge of war, years gone by, acceptance, humility. And the Lord knows — no bitterness. She glides along, scooping up new ideas, armfuls of flowers and herbs, always ready to sprinkle droplets of wisdom into the air and scatter seeds over the younger if they ask — if they want. She stands back wearing her expressions and experiences well, folding them into her cakes and sauces and between the lines of her stories...

She came from a family of six children. She tells of how they had to be filled up on soups and staples that would go a long way. Filled up on stories. Her mother was a great cook. I can imagine her, just like Wilma, constantly foraging about both outside and in. She would have searched a lifetime for those natural herbs and flowers and tidbits to slip into her loved one's palates. She would have collected endless ideas, countless cuttings

and pressed them with her spring flowers between her heaviest books and into her stores. She would have been rattling in jars and drawers and boxes to pull out bits of potential, snippings from here and there that she had tucked away for one of those grey days where she would need some reaching-into-secret-places-for-inspiration and then patchworking it all together. At night Wilma would put the children to bed and spin on into the kitchen to get on with her egg-white cake or torta campagnola for breakfast the next morning. And when she wasn't feeling fantastic she'd tie a beautiful coloured *foulard* around her neck she said, so people would be drawn to that.

This is an ode to the matriarchal figures in my life. Wilma and others who have inspired me with their stories and recipes. Their collectings and gatherings. Their offerings. They have sung well, and amongst the trousseaux they have prepared for us they have slipped in diamonds of wisdom, snippings of experience of mystery — of what to layer between our sheets, of how to hold the man down (through his stomach). They knew what was to be done, was to be done. How to make cakes people liked and splash love over the children. They knew how to roll these things off from their souls. The trousseaux, or dowry, was very common

Introduction

in Wilma's time. Passing down stories and traditions through the night. Past secrets. Recipes. Sturdy stacks of heavy oval porcelain plates and beautiful teapots. Solid casserole dishes and old silver that would carry on with candles into much of the future and mingle with lace and lavender in glowing atmospheres. There would be tips and methods to nourish this woman, passed down through her bloodline. From her mother and grandmother. The sheets would be embroidered by hand and stitched with love and memories. With experience. With the woman's initials. They were beautiful and of the finest material. Hand-picked. Hand-made. Handed down with the chests. This was the woman's value. What she brought to the marriage. To the home.

While the gentleman brought his craft, his work, his money, she brought her knowledge. Her know-how. Her art. Swimming through her veins and winding through her stitching. Spilling out into her broths. The way she had been taught. Of family. Of love. Of how to keep her home. And which herbs to use. She had the time and the *voglia* for this. And the secrets. Passed down to her, from her mother, her grandmother... I love this. These stories are our birthright. We need to lean up closer and listen. To those who have grown their own vegetables

and turned their toilings and scrapings into practical masterpieces. We need to sow our seeds, too, and be patient. Show up for the collecting when the time is right. Roll with it all. Wait. Breathe. How do we keep it? How do we hold it? We continue to swap. To collect and pass on. So they don't drift away and get forgotten. And we ask. We look for pretty tins and boxes to store these older morsels and jewels of information. And we walk with a step in the now, a step in the then and try to catch glimpses of other trousseaux as we go. We fill the chests that we will one day present to others.

Here is some inspiration I have collected. The recipes are simple and practical. They cover a multitude of uses and have at their roots a nourishing, loving and protecting clan of women. May they encourage you to pull a good roast out of the oven, stuff a chicken's neck, add an extra sugar lump, clump of herbs, peppercorns or roses to your plates and sway to the sounds of nature.

x Jessa

Many years ago, a mother would teach her daughter how to keep a home using a doll's house as an example. The daughter would learn how to make sense of it all and keep order through the various rooms. She would also be taught the art of hospitality, the times of year of celebration, how to decorate the house and, eventually, how to keep order and make sense of her own home.

To make a home that looks and smells and feels like a home — with burnished pots simmering on the stovetop and candles glowing warmly among the trousseaux linen hanging long from the tables. How to make the most of what the seasons give by preserving things. That bustling feeling through the days of the week with the various chores of washing, ironing and baking, and the harmony her know-how would bring.

SAPIENTE

WORDS/PAROLE

IF YOU DROP A KNIFE, IT MEANS
A MAN IS COMING TO VISIT.
IF YOU DROP A FORK, IT MEANS
A WOMAN IS COMING

01 *The* 12

LINEN
CUPBOARD
LA BLANCHERIA

One Week's Worth

—MONDAY—
*WASHING
DAY*

—TUESDAY—
*IRONING
DAY*

—WEDNESDAY—
*MENDING & SEWING
DAY*

—THURSDAY—
*MARKET
DAY*

—FRIDAY—
*CLEANING
DAY*

—SATURDAY—
*BAKING
DAY*

—SUNDAY—
*RESTING
DAY*

JJ

THE LIST

1 MATTRESS COVER
IN THICKER MATERIAL

1 UNDERSHEET
(IN WILMA'S DAY THEY
DIDN'T HAVE FITTED
SHEETS SO THEY WERE
EASIER TO FOLD)

1 HAND-MADE TOP
SHEET EMBROIDERED
WITH INITIALS OR
EMBLEMS

2 MATCHING
EMBROIDERED TOP
PILLOWCASES

2 PLAINER
PILLOWCASES (FOR
SECOND PILLOWS)

4 PILLOW COVERS TO
SALVAGE THE PILLOWS
BETTER

RIBBONS OF GENEROUS
LENGTHS — A COLOUR OR
PATTERN THAT WILL
REPRESENT ALL
YOUR DOUBLES

Makes 1 double bed

WILMA'S SHEETS

Wilma first had a linen shop, so she knows about these things. How to keep sheets in order. My linen cupboard used to consist of mixed piles of tablecloths, towels, single and double sheets, mismatched pillowcases, stray socks and everything else possible, all avalanching down on me.

This is what Wilma taught me for my linen cupboard. It's a wonderful method that's well worth a try. You may adjust the 'recipe' to suit your personal tastes. It is a good idea to keep some extra cut ribbons tied on a nail on the inside door of your cupboard for when you need them.

In Wilma's day, the bedcover was generally crocheted by hand or made of satin and it would cover the bed completely, keeping the sheets free of dust.

Firstly, measure your cupboard to decide how many piles of sheets can fit on a shelf. Wilma's cupboard measures 50 cm (20 inches) across so she folds her sheets to less than 25 cm (10 inches) so she can fit two piles in. Fold the freshly washed top sheet from top to bottom and then the other way — it should go four times. Then, turn and make one fold of about 20 cm (8 inches) and proceed folding the rest up like an accordion.

The finished measure is about 20 x 25 cm (8 x 10 inches) in this case. Fold the bottom sheet and mattress cover so they will be the same finished measure as the top sheet. Pillowcases are folded and kept on top of the pile and are usually smaller than the folded sheets. Once the mattress cover, undersheet, top sheet and pillowcases are all in a good and compact pile, tie this bundle together neatly with the coloured ribbon of your choice that should be used now for all doubles, and pack into your linen cupboard. Continue with the double sets. All the bundles should sit neatly on top of one another.

Proceed in the same way for single sheet sets, but with a different colour ribbon of course. Now, when you open the cupboard you will know at a glance what's what.

The same method can be used for towel sets, table linen and other sets of things.

Lasts a lifetime.

SAPIENTE
WORDS/PAROLE

USE DIFFERENT COLOURED RIBBONS TO TIE
UP SETS OF SINGLE AND DOUBLE SHEETS SO
YOU KNOW WHETHER YOU ARE ARTHUR OR
MARTHA WHEN YOU OPEN THE CUPBOARD

LINEN WATER / ACQUA DI LAVANDA

THE
LIST

2 TABLESPOONS
LAVENDER FLOWERS,
NO STALKS

1 litre (35 fl oz/4 cups)
COLD WATER

You can use dried or fresh flowers here. The stalks will colour your water, so use only the flowers. Put the scented water in a spray bottle to dampen linen when ironing for a subtle fragrance.

Wrap the lavender in a square of muslin and tie off in a tight ball. Pour the water into a bowl and add the lavender ball. Leave to sit for 20–30 minutes, removing the lavender as soon as the water begins to change colour. Pour into a spray bottle and it will keep for a long time.

JASMINE GARLANDS

A FEW BRANCHES OF
JASMINE

NEEDLE AND ENOUGH
THREAD

PATIENCE

Jasmine garlands can be made in summer. Using a needle and long thread, tack stitch them together through the base of the flowers and tie them off into long necklaces. These render a beautiful fragrance.

The Pantry

LA GIARDINIERA
(PRESERVED VEGETABLES)

LIMONCELLO

BASIL LIQUEUR

SALSA VERDE

TRUFFLE BUTTER

HERBED OILS & HERBED VINEGARS

ROSEMARY & SAGE SALT

ROSE SALT

VANILLA SALT

PEPPER SALT

STUFFED SMALL ROUND CHILLIES
WITH TUNA & ANCHOVY

RED RADICCHIO MARMALADE

NONNA'S PLUM & COGNAC MOSTARDA

CELERY MARMALADE

CHILLI & RED PEPPER JAM

ORANGE MARMALADE

PEACH JAM

QUINCE JELLY & QUINCE JAM

NONNA'S BLACKBERRIES AL NATURALE

PERFUMED SUGARS

Wise

SAPIENTE

WORDS/PAROLE

WORDS OF WISDOM

What you sow you will reap and can then heap into jars. Your work will be well rewarded through the colder months, and the jars and bottles will add a good splash of colour to the paler days and darker winter nights. They will brighten your pantry and pepper your meals. Giovanni often comes home with boxes from Wilma packaged in ways only she knows how.

SAPIENTE
WORDS/PAROLE

WORDS OF WISDOM

Mushrooms, tomatoes, onions and sauces accommodated into jars. Quinces shining like treasures from the bottom and olive oils, glistening like newly dressed soldiers, flanking the sides. And there's always a piece of cake or savoury cardoon pie that someone may have brought her, and notes and other things tucked in …

1.2 kg (2 lb 11 oz) PEPPERS
(CAPSICUMS), HALF RED
AND HALF YELLOW, STEMS
AND SEEDS REMOVED, CUT
INTO NICE CHUNKY PIECES

600 g (1 lb 5 oz/ABOUT 2)
SMALL EGGPLANTS
(AUBERGINES), HALVED OR
QUARTERED LENGTHWAYS,
THEN CUT INTO THICK SLICES

900 g (2 lb) RED BULB SPRING
ONIONS (SCALLIONS)

600 g (1 lb 5 oz) SMALL
CARROTS, SCRUBBED, WITH
SOME GREEN TOPS ATTACHED

200 g (7 oz) GREEN
BEANS, TOPPED

400 g (14 oz) FIRM
INNER CELERY STICKS
WITH SOME LEAVES

800 g (1 lb 12 oz) TRIMMED
CAULIFLOWER, CUT
INTO LARGE FLORETS

2 LONG FENNEL BULBS, CUT
LENGTHWAYS INTO 6 WEDGES
ATTACHED AT THE BASE

2 litres (70 fl oz/8 cups)
COLD WATER

500 g (1 lb 2 oz) COARSE SALT

2 litres (70 fl oz/8 cups)
WHITE WINE VINEGAR

SMALL FISTFUL OF
BLACK PEPPERCORNS

3–4 SMALL CHILLIES,
DRIED OR FRESH

2 litres (70 fl oz/8 cups)
SUNFLOWER OIL

500 ml (17 fl oz/2 cups)
OLIVE OIL

Makes a lot

PRESERVED VEGETABLES / LA GIARDINIERA

You won't believe how easy this is once you have the ingredients. You could even make a quarter of this amount.

I like to leave some of the vegetables whole or in large chunks so they look beautiful in the jars. You can use any vegetables you like, the more colours you have the merrier. The bulb spring onions from Tropea in southern Italy are a beautiful red and come in all different sizes and they are lovely in this recipe. The larger ones will have to be halved or chunked to allow the vinegar to penetrate.

Using olive oil alone will make this too heavy, so I use one part olive oil to four parts sunflower oil.

Put all the prepared vegetables in a large bucket or basin — wherever they will fit. Cover with the water, salt and vinegar and leave overnight with a weight on so they are all immersed. The next day, drain away the liquid, letting the vegetables sit for a while in a colander. You can rinse the beans now if you think they will be too salty. Cover 4 large trays with tea towels. Lay the vegetables on the trays in a single layer. Cover with a net and leave them for a few hours or even overnight.

Have cleaned, sterilised jars (see page 330) ready — as large or small as are suitable for you. Pack the vegetables compactly into the jars along with some peppercorns and at least 1 chilli in each jar. Cover with oil, starting with the sunflower oil and finishing with the olive oil. If the vegetables are not covered, just top up with more of either oil. Leave them awhile for the oils to settle, pressing out any air bubbles that may be trapped. You can put a plastic holder over the vegetables in each jar to make sure they are completely immersed in the oil. Cover with the lids and store in the pantry for at least 2–4 weeks before eating.

LIMONCELLO

8 LEMONS

1 litre (35 fl oz/4 cups)
PURE ALCOHOL (MOST
ARE BETWEEN 96–98%)

1 kg (2 lb 4 oz) SUGAR

1 litre (35 fl oz/4 cups)
WATER

———

Makes about 2.25 litres

It's such a great feeling to produce this beautiful liqueur, the colour of dusty lemons, on your very own. It is desirable to use unsprayed lemons from the Amalfi Coast, but get what you can.

We don't need the lemons here, only the skins, so I will direct you to the Lemon pie (page 296). When your limoncello is ready you can make Limoncello sorbet (page 322) or just drink it pure. This recipe is from Massimo, Giovanni's friend, and he got it from his Sicilian friend's grandmother. There you go. I love this exchanging of recipes. It's a good idea to mark the date on the carafe as you work, in case you don't remember how long the lemon peel has been macerating.

You will need a large, wide-mouthed glass carafe of 3 litres (105 fl oz/12 cups) or so.

Wash the lemons very well and scrub the skins. Pare them with a potato peeler or paring knife into good strips, taking care to only get the yellow part, not the white pith. Put them in the carafe, cover with the alcohol and leave to macerate for 1 week, covered. Give the carafe a shake every so often to make sure all the peel is covered.

Put the sugar and water in a saucepan and stir until the sugar has dissolved. Bring to the boil and simmer for just under 10 minutes. Remove from the heat. Using muslin or a fine strainer, filter the alcohol into a jug (we don't need the lemon peel any more). Slowly pour the alcohol over the hot syrup in the pan, taking care as it will spit out at you. Cool completely. Pour back into the carafe, cover again and leave for 10–15 days. It will now be ready to drink. You can pour it into smaller clear glass bottles if you like, such as the bottle the alcohol came in.

Serve well chilled (you can even keep it in the freezer). It is lovely in summer.

BASIL LIQUEUR

Marisa passed this recipe on to me and it was given to her by a contadina *who makes up many concoctions of her own. I love the way she uses a pot, even though it doesn't need any cooking. It's a great way to use up 80 leaves of basil when the plant is rolling out its leaves in abundance.*

1 litre (35 fl oz/4 cups) PURE ALCOHOL (MOST ARE BETWEEN 96–98%)

1 litre (35 fl oz/4 cups) WATER

80 BASIL LEAVES

RIND OF 4 LEMONS, YELLOW PART ONLY

800 g (1 lb 12 oz/3⅔ cup) SUGAR

——

Makes about 2.25 litres

Put everything in a pot or wide-necked carafe and cover. Leave for 1 week to 10 days, stirring it each day with a wooden spoon or giving the carafe a shake. Filter with muslin or a fine strainer into clear bottles. Use the bottle the alcohol came in if it's nice. It is ready to drink immediately. Serve it well chilled after a meal.

SALSA VERDE

This is a lovely sauce that is traditionally served with boiled meats, but it also works beautifully with grilled meats and vegetables. It will keep for a few days in the fridge but it must be covered with a layer of olive oil.

2 TABLESPOONS CHOPPED PARSLEY

2 TABLESPOONS CHOPPED TARRAGON

1 TABLESPOON CHOPPED MINT

2 GARLIC CLOVES, FINELY CHOPPED

2 TABLESPOONS DRAINED CAPERS IN VINEGAR (WITH A LITTLE VINEGAR LEFT CLINGING), CHOPPED

3 ANCHOVY FILLETS, CHOPPED

1 TEASPOON DIJON MUSTARD

160 ml (5¼ fl oz/⅔ cup) OLIVE OIL

PINCH OF GROUND CHILLI

——

Makes about ¾ cup

Put the herbs in a bowl and add the garlic, capers and anchovies. Mix the mustard and olive oil together in a small bowl, then stir this through the herb mixture. Add the chilli and a few good grinds of black pepper. Taste and adjust the seasoning as needed. Cover and put in the fridge for a while for the flavours to mingle.

SAPIENTE
WORDS/PAROLE

KEEP A FRESH WILD CHESTNUT
IN YOUR POCKET TO ENSURE YOU
DON'T CATCH A COLD

20 g (¾ oz)
WHITE TRUFFLE

30 g (1 oz)
BUTTER, SOFTENED

1 TEASPOON
OLIVE OIL

Makes about ¼ cup

TRUFFLE BUTTER

This is a luxurious butter for those wonderful times when you can get fresh truffles. I use white truffle here but you can also use black. The intensity of your truffle butter will depend on the truffle season. This is a humble amount, but if you were to make more the proportion of truffle to butter would be less. For example, if you had 200 g (7 oz) of truffles, then you would probably need about 1 kg (2 lb 4 oz) of butter. Keep any butter you don't use immediately in the freezer to preserve its strength.

You can keep your truffle (or truffles) buried in rice, then use the rice with its lingering perfume to make a risotto with butter and parmesan.

Clean the truffle (or truffles) well with a stiff brush, making sure to get rid of any attached soil. Shave or slice very finely, then chop up. Mix into the butter with the olive oil, a little salt if your butter is unsalted and a few grinds of black pepper. Keep in a closed jar in the fridge to use soon, or pat into a log and wrap in baking paper, then plastic wrap and freeze. Cut slices as needed.

HERBED OILS

THE
LIST

HERBED OILS WILL KEEP
FOR UP TO 6 MONTHS IF
IN STERILISED BOTTLES
(SEE PAGE 330)

I love having a row of bottles of oils with herbs and things dropped into them. Apart from how they look, they add depth to a salad dressing or anything that might need a splash of oil.

You can top up the oil when necessary and add extra flavourings. Just make sure the flavourings are covered with the oil. You will need a bottle with a spouted cork on top for drizzling.

Things that flavour oils nicely are garlic, chillies, fresh herbs, spices such as pink, black or green peppercorns, and even flowers like lavender and rose.

Choose an oil that is not too heavy or strong, as this could mask or clash with the flavourings added.

HERBED VINEGARS

HERBED VINEGARS WILL
KEEP FOR UP TO
6 MONTHS IF IN STERILISED
BOTTLES (SEE PAGE 330)

Wilma says that years ago, when vinegar was a bit weak or the bottle was getting low, they'd put 4 or 5 strands of uncooked spaghetti in it. The starch of the pasta helped strengthen the vinegar. They would also add the leftovers from a bottle of wine, pouring it through a paper towel to hold back any fondo. This would then make more vinegar. But you had to have the mother, the starter, in there.

To help the fermentation, they would use a piece of paper for a cork. This would allow the vinegar to breathe.

Things that nicely flavour vinegar include lemon peel, chillies, garlic, herbs such as tarragon, and spices like peppercorns, coriander seeds and allspice.

Choose a base vinegar by strength, flavour and colour. For example, you could use cider vinegar, or white or red wine vinegar, or a combination of the two for a rosé blush.

Infuse the vinegar for a week or two before using. The vinegar will last as long as the flavourings are covered.

ROSEMARY & SAGE SALT

5 TABLESPOONS
CHOPPED ROSEMARY

5 TABLESPOONS
CHOPPED SAGE

2 GARLIC CLOVES, CHOPPED

1 SMALL RED CHILLI,
CHOPPED

160 g (5½ oz/½ cup)
PINK HIMALAYAN SALT
(OR OTHER COARSE SALT)

A FEW BLACK PEPPERCORNS

Makes about 1¼ cups

This is great to always have in your kitchen, to scatter over meats and potatoes before roasting. The herbs will perfume and flavour the salt beautifully. It's up to you as to how much you use, and you can be less heavy-handed if you prefer less salt. You will need a good amount of lovely fresh rosemary and sage. Strip the leaves off their branches before chopping them.

Scatter the rosemary, sage, garlic and chilli on a tray lined with baking paper. Cover with a net and put in front of a window that gets direct sunlight.

Crush the salt in small batches in a mortar with a pestle. It's nice to have varying texture in the salt, but each crystal should be at least cracked. Crush the peppercorns with the last batch. Toss onto the tray with the herbs and leave to dry, then store in a closed jar.

ROSE SALT

160 g (5½ oz/½ cup)
PINK HIMALAYAN SALT
(OR OTHER COARSE SALT)

ABOUT 2½ TABLESPOONS
TINY, DRIED, EXQUISITELY
PERFUMED UNSPRAYED
DAMASCUS ROSES,
OR OTHER EDIBLE
ROSES OR PETALS

Makes about ¾ cup

Rose salt adds a lovely scented layer to a dish. I love having this kind of accessory sitting on my marble top for its persistent lingering perfume.

In a mortar, crush the salt in batches with a pestle until it looks like crushed diamonds. Some crystals will be fine and others still coarse, but each diamond should have been at least gently cracked so you don't have rocks on your plate. A little bite is lovely though.

Tip the salt into a bowl. Put the roses in the mortar and crush gently with the pestle to release many of the petals, but don't pulverise them. Stop when they look gorgeous and shake them out into your salt. Remove any dark inner bits that don't look great. Turn through gently. Breathe.

Keeps for many months in a tightly closed container or box. Turn through gently before using.

VANILLA SALT

THE
LIST

160 g (5½ oz/½ cup)
PINK HIMALAYAN SALT
(OR OTHER COARSE SALT)

2 PLUMP VANILLA BEANS

2 TEASPOONS VANILLA
EXTRACT

Makes about ½ cup

I love to sprinkle this over fish or salads and vegetables. These amounts are just approximate. You may make as much or as little as you like. You can also tuck in a rinsed and dried vanilla bean that you have used elsewhere.

Preheat the oven to 180°C (350°F/Gas 4).

In a mortar, pound the salt in batches with a pestle. Some salt will be fine and some will be coarse, which is perfect. Tip into a bowl. Split the vanilla beans down their length with a small sharp knife and halve. Scrape out the seeds with the tip of the knife into the salt, then scatter the vanilla extract over. Take some salt in your hands and massage the beans to get as many vanilla seeds as possible into the salt and mix the vanilla extract through. Add the vanilla bean pods.

Tip the salt onto a baking tray lined with baking paper and bake for 5–6 minutes, to dry it out. Remove from the oven and cool, then set aside until completely dry. Tip into a container or box that you can close tightly and leave for a week or two before using, turning it through every now and then so it is well distributed. Keeps for a long time.

PEPPER SALT

160 g (5½ oz/½ cup)
PINK HIMALAYAN SALT
(OR OTHER COARSE SALT)

2 TEASPOONS BLACK
PEPPERCORNS

2 TEASPOONS PINK
PEPPERCORNS

Makes about ½ cup

This is nice, easy and very convenient to have ready. I use it in the Salt & pepper potatoes with a trickle of buttermilk (page 110) and it is also lovely scattered over grilled steaks, chicken or fish.

Crush the salt in a mortar with a pestle, a bit at a time. Tip into a bowl. Crush half the peppercorns with just one crack and the rest a little more. Mix together with the salt. Store in a closed box. Give it a gentle shake before using.

STUFFED SMALL ROUND CHILLIES WITH TUNA & ANCHOVY

1.5 kg (3 lb 5 oz/ABOUT 50)
SMALL ROUND
RED CHILLIES

ABOUT 500 ml (17 fl oz/
2 cups) WHITE
WINE VINEGAR

10 BLACK PEPPERCORNS

5 WHOLE CLOVES

400 g (14 oz)
WELL-DRAINED
TINNED TUNA IN OIL

ABOUT 100 g (3½ oz)
ANCHOVY FILLETS,
WELL DRAINED

150 g (5½ oz) CAPERS IN
VINEGAR, WELL DRAINED

OLIVE OIL, TO COVER THE
CHILLIES IN THE JARS

Makes several jars

You will need wide-necked sterilised jars (see page 330) to accommodate these beauties. I hope you can find gorgeous round jewels of chillies, such as these. Small ones are a lovely monodose that you can just pop in your mouth, while bigger ones can be shared.

Use thin gloves when working with the chillies so your hands don't burn for the rest of the day.

The amount of filling you'll need will vary, depending on the size of your chillies. Mine were all different, which looks lovely in the jar. Just make up extra filling if needed, and if you have too much serve the leftovers on crostini.

Cover a couple of baking trays with clean tea towels. Rinse the chillies. Put the vinegar in a not-too-wide pot — you will need enough to just cover the chillies. Bring to the boil, then add the peppercorns and cloves, and dive in the chillies in batches so they all get a full chance in the vinegar. Let it come back to the boil and then boil for 3 or 4 minutes, but no more. Remove to the lined trays with a slotted spoon (return any peppercorns or cloves to the vinegar), then add the next batch to the vinegar and so on, until they are all done. Leave to cool.

Use a small sharp knife to cut out the hat of each chilli without piercing or removing any flesh. As you pull the hat away many of the seeds will come with it, but you will need a very small teaspoon to remove the rest of the seeds, taking special care not to break the chillies. Best to sit down and relax while you do this, with a dustbin in front of you and thin gloves on your hands. Arrange the chillies back on the tray for now. You can discard the seeds or you might like to plant them.

Put the tuna, anchovies and capers on a board and chop them well, but not completely smooth; some texture is good. You can pulse them in a food processor if you like. Mix them together to make a well-combined paste.

Now, fill the chillies. Holding a chilli in one hand (again wearing gloves), grab some of the paste and stuff it into the belly of the chilli, pressing down well with your fingers so it is tight and firmly packed, nearly flush. Carefully put the stuffed chillies in the jars, sitting them upright and nestled close to one another. Gently pour olive oil over them, then wait for the level to settle and add more as necessary to completely cover the chillies. You can put a plastic holder on top to keep the chillies submerged.

The chillies will need a few weeks in the jar before serving for the flavours to mix well. The jars can be kept on a shelf in the pantry until opened, then put them in the fridge. The oil will congeal but it needs just a short while at room temperature to return to its glossy old self.

RED RADICCHIO MARMALADE

This is great with mature pecorino or other cheeses. It also works well with boiled meats and is particularly nice with game. Lovely with sausages, too.

Quarter the radicchio and remove the thick white stems. Shred the leaves, not too coarsely. Heat the oil in a wide heavy-bottomed pot and sauté the radicchio until it has surrendered a bit. Add the rest of the ingredients, some salt and a few grinds of black pepper. Simmer, partly covered, for about 1½ hours, until it has reduced and is thick and a bit jammy looking. Remove the lid and simmer for another 30 minutes or until most of the liquid has gone, stirring often. Ladle into warm sterilised jars (see page 330), seal with the lids and turn upside down. Leave to cool before turning upright, creating a vacuum. Store in the pantry until opened, then keep in the fridge.

THE
LIST

1 kg (2 lb 4 oz) ROUND
RED RADICCHIO

4 TABLESPOONS OLIVE OIL

600 g (1 lb 5 oz) SUGAR

250 ml (9 fl oz/1 cup) WATER

250 ml (9 fl oz/1 cup)
RED WINE

2½ TABLESPOONS
BALSAMIC VINEGAR

2½ TABLESPOONS FRESHLY
SQUEEZED LEMON JUICE

40 g (1½ oz) ZIBBIBO RAISINS OR
SMALL SEEDLESS MUSCATELS

1 BAY LEAF

A GOOD FEW PINCHES
OF GROUND CHILLI

2 APPLES, CORED AND
COARSELY GRATED

Makes about 4 cups

SAPIENTE
WORDS/PAROLE

THE FAT IN MILK WORKS WELL
AS A SHOE POLISH SUBSTITUTE.
RUB A LITTLE MILK WITH A CLOTH
ONTO YOUR LEATHER SHOES TO
CLEAN AND POLISH THEM

NONNA'S PLUM & COGNAC MOSTARDA

THE
LIST

1 kg (2 lb 4 oz) PLUMS

700 g (1 lb 9 oz) SUGAR

1 CINNAMON STICK

50 g (1¾ oz) MUSTARD POWDER

125 ml (4 fl oz/½ cup)
COGNAC

Makes 4 cups

This is good to make when plums are at their best, so you can enjoy their flavour for the rest of the year. It is lovely next to roasted meats or even cold meats and cheeses.

Halve the plums and discard the stones. Put the plum halves in a large bowl, scatter the sugar over and leave for 12 hours, covered with a tea towel.

Scrape everything into a metal pot and bring slowly to the boil, stirring often. Boil, uncovered, for 10 minutes. Remove from the heat and allow to cool, then cover. After 12 hours, add the cinnamon stick and then boil again, uncovered, for 10 minutes. Remove from the heat, allow to cool and leave, covered, for another 12 hours.

Mix the mustard and cognac together in a small bowl, then stir this through the plums. Bring to the boil and simmer, uncovered, for about 15 minutes or until a teaspoonful dropped onto a plate clings, rather than runs, when the plate is tilted. Overcooking will make the mostarda too firm. Bottle while hot into warm sterilised jars (see page 330). Seal with the lids and turn upside down. Leave to cool before turning upright, creating a vacuum. Store in the pantry until opened, then keep in the fridge.

CELERY
MARMALADE

THE
LIST

1 BUNCH CELERY, ABOUT
1.7 kg (3 lb 12 oz)

1 kg (2 lb 4 oz) SUGAR

GOOD PINCH OF CHILLI FLAKES

FINELY GRATED RIND OF
1 LEMON, YELLOW PART ONLY

JUICE OF 1 LEMON

150 ml (5 fl oz) WHITE WINE

150 ml (5 fl oz) WATER

3 TABLESPOONS GRAPPA

Makes 4 cups

This is beautiful with a mixed cheese plate and alongside ham. The grappa is there to keep the good green colour, says Wilma. It's a good idea to fill various small jars so they don't stay open for too long in the fridge.

Wash and trim the celery, and cut into sticks. You will need 300 g (10½ oz) of inner ones with their leaves and 700 g (1 lb 9 oz) of thick outer ones. Leave the inner ones to one side for now. String the thick sticks with a small, sharp paring knife by digging in at one end of the stick, then lifting the strings and dragging them down. Strip all the strings away or they will just end up in your marmalade. Chop up roughly, then blitz in a food processor, but don't make it too fine as some small bits are good.

The tender inner sticks probably won't need stripping. Slice these and their leaves into rounds so they will show up in your jars. Put all the celery in a suitable pot with the sugar, chilli flakes, lemon rind and juice, wine and water, and bring to a gentle boil. Lower the heat and simmer, uncovered, stirring extremely often to check that nothing is sticking or caramelising. If it seems to be going along too quickly and the sugar is getting ahead of the celery, add a little more water. Continue simmering and stirring for 45 minutes to an hour, until it is a bit jammy but still loose.

To test when it is ready, drop a teaspoonful onto a small saucer and tilt. It shouldn't slide down easily, but drag with a little resistance. Add the grappa and let it cook for a couple of minutes more, then turn off the heat. Ladle into warm sterilised jars (see page 330). Seal the lids tightly and turn the jars upside down. Leave to cool before turning upright, creating a vacuum. Store in the pantry until opened, then keep in the fridge.

CHILLI & RED PEPPER JAM

1 kg (2 lb 4 oz) BRIGHT RED
PEPPERS (CAPSICUMS)

240 g (8½ oz) SMALL
RED CHILLIES

1.15 kg (2 lb 8½ oz)
SUGAR

1½ TABLESPOONS
RED WINE VINEGAR

125 ml (4 fl oz/½ cup)
WATER

Makes about 5 cups

This is sweet and hot, a beautiful thing to whip out and serve next to almost anything. Its strength will depend on the type of chillies you use. Choose ones that are soft, a beautiful red and not drying out. I like to use jars of varying sizes. Be sure to label them so you remember what's inside.

Remove the stems and seeds from the peppers. Roughly cut up the flesh directly into a large heavy-based pot. Wearing gloves, remove the tops from the chillies, then slice them lengthways and scrape out the seeds. You will need about 150 g (5½ oz) of cleaned chillies, depending on their strength. Take extreme care when working with chillies that the seeds are not flying all over the kitchen and remember not to touch your skin or eyes, as it can burn for ages. Rinse, then cut them up roughly and put in the pot. It's okay if a few seeds go in.

Add the sugar, vinegar and water and bring to the boil, then slightly lower the heat to a steady simmer. Partly cover and simmer for about an hour to soften the chillies. Pulse until smooth with a hand-held blender directly in the pot. Return to the heat and simmer, uncovered, for 15 minutes or longer if necessary to thicken up slightly. To test when the marmalade is ready, drop a teaspoonful onto a small saucer and tilt. It should not slip down easily, but slide with a little resistance.

Have warm sterilised jars (see page 330) ready for filling. Funnel the jam in, or ladle it into a jug and then pour into the jars, taking care not to burn yourself. Put the lids on, close tightly and then turn the jars upside down. Leave to cool before turning upright, creating a vacuum. Store in the pantry until opened, then keep in the fridge.

SAPIENTE
WORDS/PAROLE

TO CLEAN DEPOSITS FROM THE BOTTOM
OF BOTTLES, POUR IN SOME COARSE SALT,
A HANDFUL OF RICE, SOME VINEGAR AND
A LITTLE WARM WATER. SHAKE WELL

ORANGE
MARMALADE

THE
LIST

2 kg (4 lb 8 oz) ORANGES

1 LEMON

1.2 kg (2 lb 10 oz) SUGAR

3 TABLESPOONS COGNAC

Makes about 6 cups

Try to get seedless oranges to save you the step of removing the pips. Use unsprayed oranges and scrub the skins well beforehand.

Prick the oranges all over with a toothpick, put in a large pot and cover with warm water. Cut the rind off the lemon in thin strips and add to the oranges, along with the juice of the lemon. Leave for 12 hours.

Drain the oranges and cut away their top hats. Cut them into thin slices, then cut those into quarters. Put in a large heavy-based pot, add the sugar and leave to macerate, covered, for 12 hours. Now, put the pot over a low flame and bring to the boil. Simmer, uncovered, for 1½ hours, then add 750 ml (26 fl oz/3 cups) of hot water. Simmer for another 1½ hours, adding another 750 ml or so of hot water during this time as the marmalade reduces. The peel should be translucent and tender, and there should be a nice amount of thickened liquid.

To test when it is ready, drop a teaspoonful onto a small saucer and tilt. It should not slip down easily, but slide with a little resistance. Add the cognac and simmer for a few minutes more before removing from the heat. Distribute among warm sterilised jars (see page 330), seal with the lids and turn upside down. Leave to cool before turning upright, creating a vacuum. Store in the pantry until opened, then keep in the fridge.

1 kg (2 lb 4 oz) RIPE PEACHES

500 g (1 lb 2 oz) SUGAR

2 TABLESPOONS AMARETTO

Makes about 4 cups

PEACH
JAM

Many ladies I have questioned say that peach jam is their favourite. This is a lovely recipe, with just three ingredients. It is quite a loose jam and I like it that way. Serve it with bread for breakfast or use it to fill a crostata.

The peaches must be sweet and ripe. Keep a few of the peach stones to add to your jam while it cooks, as these give another layer of flavour.

Halve the peaches, leaving the skins on. Remove the stones, keeping about 4 aside. Put the peaches in a pot suitable for making jam and cover with 250 ml (9 fl oz/ 1 cup) of water. Put the lid on and simmer for about 20 minutes to soften the peaches. Pulse with a hand-held blender directly in the pot until smooth. Now, add the sugar and the saved stones. Bring back to the boil, then lower the heat and simmer for about 1 hour, stirring with a wooden spoon very regularly to check that nothing is sticking. Do the plate test; drop a teaspoonful onto a small saucer and tilt. It should not slip down easily, but cling.

When the jam is ready add the amaretto and cook for a couple of minutes more. Ladle into warm sterilised jars (see page 330), seal with the lids and turn upside down. Leave to cool before turning upright, creating a vacuum. Store in the pantry until opened, then keep in the fridge.

SAPIENTE
WORDS/PAROLE

QUINCES CAN BE KEPT IN THE LINEN
CUPBOARD FOR THE LOVELY FRAGRANCE
THEY GIVE (IN A BOWL SO THEY
DON'T STAIN ANYTHING)

QUINCE JELLY

THE
LIST

2 kg (4 lb 8 oz)
RIPE QUINCES

1 LEMON

ABOUT 550 g (1 lb 4 oz/
2½ cups) SUGAR

Makes 3 cups

The quinces in this recipe can be cooked in a pressure cooker, which would reduce the cooking time by around a third and maintain a good water level, too. Wilma doesn't let anything go to waste and uses the cooked pulp to make Quince jam (see opposite).

Cut the quinces into small chunks, cores and all, and the lemon into quarters. Put them all in a deep pot and cover with plenty of water. Bring to the boil and simmer gently, partly covered, until the fruit is soft and the liquid is a lovely fuchsia pink. This can take anywhere from 2 hours on, so check often by piercing the fruit with a small sharp knife. Resist the temptation to add extra water during cooking.

Wet and wring out a jelly bag or line a large colander with damp muslin and sit it over a bowl. Pour in the fruit and leave, without stirring or pressing, until all the juice has run through. Overnight is good.

Measure the juice, then pour it into a large enamel or stainless-steel pan. (Save the quince pulp to make jam, but discard the lemon quarters.) Weigh out 550 g (1 lb 4 oz) of sugar for every 1 litre (35 fl oz/4 cups) of juice and add to the pan. Stir over medium heat until the sugar has dissolved, then bring to the boil. Skim any scum from the surface.

Simmer, uncovered, until the setting point is reached, about 45 minutes. To check if it's ready, dab a little between your fingers and pull them slowly apart — the jelly should form a slightly sticky string. Pour into warm sterilised jars (see page 330). Seal well, turn upside down and leave to cool. Turn the jars upright, creating a vacuum. Store in the pantry until opened, then keep in the fridge.

QUINCE JAM

COOKED QUINCE PULP
(PRECEDING PAGE)

ABOUT 800 g (1 lb 12 oz/
3²/₃ cups) SUGAR

125 ml (4 fl oz/½ cup)
RED WINE

GRATED RIND, YELLOW
PART ONLY, OF 1 LEMON

JUICE OF 1 LEMON

———

Makes 5–6 cups

Remove the cores and seeds from the quince pulp. Put the quinces through a ricer or mash with a potato masher. Weigh the purée and allow 600 g (1 lb 5 oz) sugar for every 1 kg (2 lb 4 oz). Put the sugar, purée, wine and lemon rind and juice in a heavy-based pan. Bring to the boil, then simmer slowly for 30 minutes, stirring almost continuously, until you have a lovely thick jam. It is important that it is on low heat and that you stir regularly so that it doesn't catch.

Do the plate test; drop a teaspoonful onto a saucer and tilt. The jam should cling rather than slip down easily, and it should wrinkle when poked. Pour into warm sterilised jars (see page 330). Seal with the lids and turn upside down. Leave to cool before turning upright, creating a vacuum. Store in the pantry until opened, then keep in the fridge

NONNA'S BLACKBERRIES AL NATURALE

500 g (1 lb 2 oz)
BLACKBERRIES,
CLEANED AND DRIED
WITH PAPER TOWELS

4 TABLESPOONS
SUGAR

———

Makes 2 x 750 ml jars

This is a great way to keep blackberries going a little longer, or any fruits really — cherries, grapes, plums in pieces and so on. I like them like this, not too sweet, though you can use more sugar if you like. They are wonderful al naturale or served with a scoop of Fior di latte ice cream (page 323).

Put the blackberries in two 750 ml (26 fl oz/3 cup) jars. The volume collapses a lot during cooking so don't press down and squash them. Scatter 2 tablespoons of sugar into each jar, then seal. Bring a large pot of water to the boil. Wrap the jars in cloths, secured with string, to avoid them clunking around. Keep the ends of the string long and use them to lower the jars into the water — the water must cover them so add more boiling water if necessary. Cover with a heavy plate to keep the jars submerged and boil for about 15 minutes. Turn off the heat and leave the jars in the water to cool completely, creating a vacuum. Store in the pantry until opened, then keep in the fridge, but not for too long.

Each recipe makes ½ cup

PERFUMED SUGARS

Scented sugars are a wonderful addition to any kitchen and are simple to make. Here are a few examples. They can be used in creams, biscuits, cakes or just scattered over fruit salads.

LAVENDER SUGAR

125 g (4½ oz) SUGAR

1 TEASPOON UNSPRAYED LAVENDER FLOWERS

Beautiful for making biscuits or whipping into a cream.

Put the sugar and lavender in a box and shake gently, like you're shaking maracas. Leave for a couple of weeks, shaking the box every now and then. When you are getting really good at the shaking, the lavender should have perfumed the sugar. You can use the sugar with the lavender in it, or sift it out if you prefer.

ROSE SUGAR

125 g (4½ oz) SUGAR

1 HANDFUL OF DRIED, FRAGRANT UNSPRAYED ROSE PETALS

Use petals with a lovely scent that you have dried well.

Put the sugar over the petals in a bowl and turn through. Cover with a net or similar to allow air to flow through. Leave for a week or so for the petals to perfume the sugar before using.

LEMON VERBENA SUGAR

125 g (4½ oz) SUGAR

18 LEMON VERBENA LEAVES

Pick the fragrant verbena leaves, spread them over a tray and leave to dry for a few days.

Put the sugar and dried leaves in a lovely tin and shake. Leave for a couple of weeks to perfume, shaking the tin every now and then. You can leave the verbena in the sugar until you use it.

— CAPITOLO —

3

The Bread Oven

CIABATTA (SOUL DOUGH)

POLISH PUFF PASTRY

FAST FOCACCIA WITH STRAWBERRIES

EMILY'S BREAD

PIZZA MARGHERITA

LA PIZZA FRITTA

SWEET PIZZA

DONZELLE

HAM & GREEN OLIVE TART

PAN DI ROSMARINO

✳

THE
————— LIST —————

QUICK STARTER (MADRE)

12 g (¼ oz) FRESH YEAST

310 ml (10¾ fl oz/1¼ cups)
TEPID WATER

300 g (10½ oz/2 cups)
BREAD (STRONG) FLOUR

1 TEASPOON SUGAR

THE REST

300 g (10½ oz/2 cups)
BREAD (STRONG) FLOUR

1 TABLESPOON OLIVE OIL

185 ml (6 fl oz/¾ cup) WATER

1 TEASPOON SALT

———

Makes 2 loaves

CIABATTA (SOUL DOUGH)

*Giovanni said 'soul dough' instead of sourdough once
– it's a perfect description. Ciabatta is my soul dough.
    There are longer routes to ciabatta. This is quite quick.
I love this bread for its irregular shape, the flour that stays
on the lovely crust and its spacious interior. It is great cut
into panini and stuffed with various fillings, such as the
Baked crumbed chicken (page 171).*

For the starter, crumble the yeast into the water in a deep
sturdy bowl. Add the flour and sugar and mix together
with a wooden spoon to a nice sloppy dough (it will be too
sticky to use your hands). Cover with plastic wrap, then a
tea towel and leave in a warm draught-free spot for an hour
or longer, until it has puffed and is bubbly.

Add the rest of the ingredients and mix in initially with
the wooden spoon. The dough will be very sticky, but resist
the temptation to add more flour. When everything is
combined use floured hands to pull and slap it around in
the bowl until springy, 1–2 minutes. It will be too sticky to
knead. Cover and leave again until full of air and puffy,
a good 2 hours or more.

Line a baking tray with baking paper and scatter a good
handful of flour over it. Scatter flour over a big wooden
board and make a little pile to the side. Press your hands in
this to cover them with flour, then divide the dough in half.
Just use the flour that is on the board and what you bring
over on your hands. Stretch and pat each half into a long
flat loaf, about 30 cm (12 inches) long and 15 cm (6 inches)
wide more or less, you want it to be lovely and irregular.
Carefully put the breads on the prepared tray, allowing for
expansion, and scatter a little extra flour on top. Cover with
a high cake net (or a similar structure that will allow for the
bread's expansion without touching it) and then a tea towel.
Leave in a warm spot for 1–1½ hours, until nice and puffy.

Preheat the oven to 210°C (415°F/Gas 6–7). Bake the
loaves until crusty and lightly golden, about 25 minutes.
Remove from the oven and transfer to a wire rack so the
crust stays crisp as the bread cools. Each ciabatta can
be cut into four for panini, if you like.

POLISH PUFF PASTRY

250 g (9 oz/1⅔ cups) PLAIN (ALL-PURPOSE) FLOUR

LARGE PINCH OF SALT

200 g (7 oz) BUTTER, CHILLED AND DICED

120 ml (4 fl oz) COLD WATER

Makes about 520 g (1 lb 2½ oz)

This isn't as hard to make as its reputation holds. You can drink a cup of herbal tea in between each chilling time and get on with whatever you are doing. The result is soft, wonderful, layered, buttery and well worth it. Incidentally, this recipe comes from Olga, the Ukrainian-Polish housekeeper who was looking after Marzia's elderly mum. In addition to her pastry making, Olga is known for having hands of gold — wonderful at working lace, darning and mending small details no-one else can do.

Pile the flour in a heap in a wide bowl and add the salt. Put the butter around the outside of the flour, tossing it very lightly in the outskirts to lightly coat. Make a well in the centre of the flour and carefully pour in the water, working it in with one hand as you pour but without incorporating any butter. Keep mixing with your hand in a stirring motion until you have a soft dough. Now, use both hands to work in the butter. If it seems to be melting before it is incorporated, use a large fork to work it in. Knead until you have a soft, smooth-ish dough — it doesn't matter if a few small unmelted bits of butter remain. Shape it into a flat block, wrap in plastic wrap and put in the fridge for 20 minutes or so.

On a lightly floured board roll the dough out to a long rectangle of about 24 x 10 cm (9½ x 4 inches). Fold one end up two-thirds of the way, then the other end down to cover it, forming a *portafoglio* (purse). Put back in the fridge, covered with plastic wrap, for 20 minutes or until it is firm. Have a rest, a cup of herbal tea. Put the dough on the board, pointing in the same direction as before, then give it a half turn so that the folded ends are now at the sides. Roll out as before. Continue like this for a total of 6 times, each time chilling it for 20 minutes or so, covered with plastic wrap. Rest some more. Have another cup of herbal tea. As you progress the dough will become smoother and easier to roll. You might find that some butter remains unincorporated, but don't worry — the main thing is to end up with a neat block of pastry with uniformly multiple layers.

Use immediately or keep in the fridge, covered, for 24 hours. Otherwise store in the freezer, then defrost in the fridge. I use this for the Chicken breast pie (page 173) and the Ham & green olive tart (page 65), and it can also be used for desserts.

20 g (¾ oz) FRESH YEAST

310 ml (10¾ fl oz/1¼ cups)
WARM WATER

4 HEAPED TABLESPOONS SUGAR

400 g (14 oz/2⅔ cups)
BREAD (STRONG) FLOUR

PINCH OF SALT

2 TABLESPOONS OLIVE OIL

500 g (1 lb 2 oz) STRAWBERRIES

ICING (CONFECTIONERS')
SUGAR, TO SERVE

FAST FOCACCIA WITH STRAWBERRIES

This is truly lovely. The kind of thing you like just being at the same table with. The strawberries must be incredible – sweet and bursting with flavour. If yours are not, you may need more sugar. You can serve this as a snack or for breakfast, it's something between a sweet and a bread.

Crumble the yeast into a large bowl and stir in the water with 1 heaped tablespoon of the sugar. Add the flour and salt and knead lightly, dipping your hands in a little flour if necessary, to give a soft, stickier than usual dough.

Flick a little water over a good-sized baking tray (about 33 x 30 cm/13 x 12 inches). Line with a piece of baking paper, ironing the paper down with your hands so it sticks. Dribble the olive oil on and spread this over the paper (with your hands if you like, for your skin to benefit from the great properties of olive oil). Now put the dough on the tray and begin to spread it to completely cover the tray. It probably won't cooperate immediately, so stretch it to perhaps halfway, then leave it for 5 minutes or so and go back to it after its rest. Stretch and press it with your palms to edge it out to the sides of the tray. Cover with a high cake net if you have one and then a tea towel, or a similar system so that the dough won't touch the cloth. Leave it in a warm draught-free place to rise, about 1–1½ hours.

Meanwhile, rinse the strawberries and remove their green hats. Leave small ones whole, halve medium-sized ones and cut large ones into thirds. Put them in a bowl and scatter with 2 heaped tablespoons of sugar. Turn them through gently and leave at room temperature, covered.

Preheat the oven to 200°C (400°F/Gas 6). When the dough has puffed up nicely, gently turn the strawberries again, being careful not to break or mash them. Quickly and gently, so the dough doesn't deflate, place them all over the dough, keeping most of them upright so they look good once baked. Dribble the juices here and there as you go. Scatter the last heaped tablespoon of sugar evenly over the top, right to the sides. Bake for about 25 minutes or until the focaccia is golden and crisp on the edges and the strawberries have a lovely juicy look about them, almost scorched on a few edges. Make sure the middle part is cooked too, turning the tray around if necessary for the last 5 minutes. Don't overcook or the strawberries will collapse into a jam. Remove. Cool. Shake icing sugar over the top. Cut off pieces with kitchen scissors. Eat.

SAPIENTE

WORDS/PAROLE

FIRST DESERVE,
THEN DESIRE

EMILY'S BREAD

THE
LIST

25 g (1 oz) FRESH YEAST

250 ml (9 fl oz/1 cup)
TEPID WATER

1 TEASPOON SUGAR

2 TABLESPOONS
PLAIN YOGHURT

2 TABLESPOONS OLIVE OIL

3 TABLESPOONS COOLED
ESPRESSO COFFEE

500 g (1 lb 2 oz) MANITOBA
FLOUR OR BREAD
(STRONG) FLOUR

½ TEASPOON SALT

Makes 2 loaves

*I just love the idea of this simple bread. I can picture
Emily, picking up the breakfast things after everyone has
vanished and then tipping all the leftovers into her baking
bowl. How wonderfully wild. But yes, why throw these
things out when you can produce a couple of loaves
for the next meal?*

Crumble the yeast into a large deep bowl and whisk in the
water and sugar. When the yeast begins to bubble add
the yoghurt, olive oil and coffee and mix with a wooden
spoon to combine. Mix in the flour and then the salt to
form a rather soft dough. Add a little more water or flour
as necessary. Knead lightly for a few minutes in the bowl.
Cover with a tea towel and leave in a warm, draught-free
place until well puffed up, about 1½ hours.

Line a large baking tray with baking paper. Knock the
dough down and divide into 2 portions. Shape into rather
elongated loaves and make 3 diagonal slashes across
each one. Put them on the lined tray, leaving a good
space in between. Cover again and leave in the warm
spot until puffed and risen, about 1 hour.

Preheat the oven to 200°C (400°F/Gas 6). Bake the
loaves for 20–25 minutes, until golden and crusty both
underneath and on top. Remove to a wire rack to cool.

This bread still tastes very good the next day and is
also great toasted.

PIZZA MARGHERITA

25 g (1 oz) FRESH YEAST

JUST UNDER 280 ml (9½ fl oz)
TEPID WATER

PINCH OF SUGAR

500 g (1 lb 2 oz/3⅓ cups)
BREAD (STRONG) FLOUR

1 TEASPOON SALT

2 X 400 g (14 oz) TINS
CHOPPED TOMATOES

4 TABLESPOONS OLIVE OIL

ABOUT 6 BASIL LEAVES

250 g (9 oz) FRESH MOZZARELLA

—————

*Makes 2 pizzas
(+ 4 fried pizzas, see opposite)*

There is something incredibly refreshing about a pizza margherita. You can't go wrong if your ingredients are beautiful. Its lovely name comes from Queen Margherita — it is said that when she was visiting Napoli the pizzaiolo made this pizza in her honour. You can use buffalo mozzarella in place of the regular mozzarella if you like. There will be enough dough for 4 pizzas, but I have only made 2 pizzas and used the rest for La pizza fritta (see opposite). If you need to keep any unused dough, wrap it in plastic wrap and store in the fridge overnight, or in the freezer.

Crumble the yeast into a small bowl and add the water and sugar. Put the flour in a large mixing bowl and make a well in the centre. When the yeast starts to bubble, pour it into the flour. Mix with your hands to get a smooth soft dough, adding a little more water or flour as necessary. Mix in the salt, then knead the dough until very smooth and elastic, at least 5 minutes. Divide the dough equally between 2 bowls (you will have roughly 400 g/14 oz in each bowl), cover each with a tea towel and leave in a warm place to rise for about an hour or until well puffed.

Meanwhile, tip the tomatoes into a bowl (I like some chunks here), add 2 tablespoons of the olive oil and season with salt and black pepper. Tear 2 basil leaves in, mix through and leave aside at room temperature, covered for now. Cut the mozzarella into slices and then into small blocks, leaving it on a tilted plate at room temperature so much of its liquid drains off.

Take one of the bowls, punch down the dough and divide it into 2 balls. Cover them with a tea towel so they don't dry out (*pizzaioli* keep them in a drawer) and leave to rise again for about 20 minutes. Preheat the oven to 220°C (425°F/Gas 7).

Very lightly oil two 31 cm (12½ inch) diameter pizza trays. Put a ball of dough on each tray. Using your palms and fingertips, press each ball of dough from the middle outwards, to extend it to the edges of the tray. Sometimes this is easier if you take it halfway, let it rest for 5 minutes or so and then finish taking it to the edge — it will move better after its rest. Dollop 1 cup of tomato onto the centre of each pizza (the leftover tomato is for La pizza fritta).

Using the back of the ladle like the *pizzaioli* do, spread the sauce from the middle outwards. Drizzle a tablespoon of olive oil over the top and put the trays in the oven.

Bake until the edges are golden in places and the underneath of the pizza is firm, not flabby and pale, about 15 minutes. Depending on your oven, it may be necessary to swap the trays around halfway through. If you prefer, you can roll out and bake the pizzas one at a time. Take out the pizzas, scatter the mozzarella over them and put back in the oven until the mozzarella melts, about 5 minutes. Serve hot, with a couple of fresh basil leaves scattered on top.

LA PIZZA FRITTA

THE
LIST

½ BATCH (400 g/14 oz)
RISEN PIZZA DOUGH
(PRECEDING RECIPE)

LIGHT OLIVE OIL,
FOR FRYING

THE REMAINING TOMATO FROM
THE PRECEDING RECIPE, ABOUT
¾ cup, AT ROOM TEMPERATURE

200 g (7 oz) FRESH MOZZARELLA,
AT ROOM TEMPERATURE,
IN 1 cm (½ inch) SLICES

A FEW BASIL LEAVES

Makes 4

Maybe we all look as good frying pizzas as Sophia Loren in the movie L'Oro di Napoli *(The Gold of Naples)?*

The cheese here doesn't get cooked so it is worth trying buffalo mozzarella or burrata, a very creamy fresh mozzarella, if you can get it. Otherwise, use a good-quality fresh mozzarella. These pizzas are surprisingly light.

Divide the dough into 4 equal balls. On a lightly floured board pat each one out to a rough oval shape of about 20 x 15 cm (8 x 6 inches). Pour enough oil into a wide frying pan to cover the bottom.

Heat the oil and add the pizzas two at a time if they fit but if not, one by one. Fry until golden underneath, then turn and fry the other side until golden but not too dark. Remove with tongs and put on a plate lined with paper towels to drain. Immediately dollop some tomato on top, leaving the border free as one does with pizza, and top at once with mozzarella slices so they soften from the heat. Scatter a couple of basil leaves over and serve hot hot.

LONG AGO, WHEN THERE WERE
NO SUCH THINGS AS TIMERS,
IF SOMEONE ASKED HOW LONG
SOMETHING WOULD NEED IN
THE OVEN, THE ANSWER MAY
HAVE BEEN 'AS LONG AS IT
TAKES TO RECITE THREE
"AVE MARIAS"' — AND THEN IT
WOULD BE ABOUT READY

½ BATCH RISEN PIZZA DOUGH
(PAGE 56), ABOUT 400 g (14 oz)

150 g (5½ oz) RASPBERRIES

1 TABLESPOON SUGAR

35 g (1¼ oz) SKINNED
HAZELNUTS, HALVED

4 TABLESPOONS CHOCOLATE
SPREAD (PAGE 276), OR
A BOUGHT ONE

ICING (CONFECTIONERS')
SUGAR, TO SERVE

Makes 2 pizzas

SWEET PIZZA

I've seen many Italians enjoying a sweet pizza after a savoury one, even if it's just a slice. They make a lovely sweet finish to a meal and are great for sharing.

Preheat the oven to 200°C (400°F/Gas 6). Very lightly oil two 31 cm (12½ inch) diameter pizza trays. Divide the dough in half and put each portion on a tray. Using your palms and fingertips, press each portion of dough from the middle outwards to extend it to the edges of the tray. Sometimes this is easier if you take it halfway, let it rest for 5 minutes or so and then finish taking it to the edge — it will move better after its rest.

Scatter the raspberries over one base and sprinkle with the sugar. The other base stays plain for now. Put both trays in the oven and bake for 10–12 minutes or until golden, swapping the trays around halfway through.

Meanwhile, toast the hazelnuts with a light sprinkling of salt in a dry frying pan. Remove the trays from the oven. Dollop the chocolate spread over the plain base and spread gently with the back of the spoon, not quite all the way to the edge. Scatter the hazelnuts over. Dust the raspberry pizza with icing sugar and serve both warm.

DONZELLE

½ BATCH RISEN PIZZA DOUGH (PAGE 56), ABOUT 400 g (14 oz)

LIGHT OLIVE OIL, FOR FRYING

6–8 THIN SLICES OF PROSCIUTTO, WITHOUT TOO MUCH FAT

ABOUT 150 g (5½ oz) STRACCHINO CHEESE, AT ROOM TEMPERATURE

Makes 12–14

Everyone seems to love these fried puffs, which are often made spontaneously from excess pizza or bread dough. They must be served hot and plain with a light sprinkling of salt. They make a fine meal or a starter, served in a basket with a plate of sliced prosciutto and another of stracchino to fill them. Stracchino is a soft fresh rindless cow's milk cheese that has a mild taste. You need to have a generous amount of oil in the pan for the donzelle to cook properly. Sometimes they are served with a good shaking of icing sugar instead of salt.

Tear off pieces of dough and roll out or shape them into rough squares of 4 x 5 cm (1½ x 2 inches), or roll to make cigars. Leave to rise, covered (the timing is not important). You can shape or roll and fry as you go, so you have some dough rising while you're preparing and frying others.

Heat enough oil in a wide pan to cover the base. Gently drop the puffs in the hot oil in batches and fry until golden on both sides. Remove with tongs to a tray lined with paper towels. Scatter a few grains of salt over each and serve immediately with the prosciutto and stracchino. Eat them split and filled like a panino or with the fillings draped on top, or serve them simply sprinkled with salt.

SAPIENTE

WORDS/PAROLE

BLOSSOM WHERE
YOU ARE PLANTED

HAM & GREEN OLIVE TART

THE
LIST

250 g (9 oz) POLISH PUFF
PASTRY (PAGE 51)

3 EGGS

250 ml (9 fl oz/1 cup) POURING
(WHIPPING) CREAM

50 g (1¾ oz) FRESHLY
GRATED PARMESAN

150 g (5½ oz) THINLY SLICED
HAM, ROUGHLY CHOPPED

120 g (4¼ oz) PITTED GREEN
OLIVES, QUARTERED OR
HALVED IF NOT VERY BIG

ABOUT 1 TEASPOON THYME
LEAVES, PLUS THYME SPRIGS TO
SCATTER ON TOP IF YOU LIKE

Serves 6

This is lovely with a nice big salad, as the start to a meal or even a light lunch. I like the ham and green olives together, but you really could add anything you like.

Preheat the oven to 180°C (350°F/Gas 4). Butter a round 24 cm (9½ inch) springform tin. On a large sheet of baking paper roll out the pastry to a 34 cm (13½ inch) circle. Use to line the tin, with the pastry coming two-thirds of the way up the side.

Whip the eggs in a bowl, then mix in the cream, parmesan, ham, olives and thyme. Add a few grindings of black pepper and mix it all well. Scrape out into the pastry, pushing the ham and olives around with the tip of a spoon to fill any empty spaces. Bake for about 35 minutes or until the top is golden here and there, and set. Don't overcook it, but make sure the pastry is golden around the edges, well cooked and crisp underneath.

Cool a bit before cutting. I like this tart warm but it can also be eaten at room temperature.

PAN DI ROSMARINO

12 g (¼ oz) FRESH YEAST

½ TEASPOON RUNNY HONEY

250 ml (9 fl oz/1 cup)
TEPID WATER

500 g (1 lb 2 oz/3⅓ cups)
BREAD (STRONG) FLOUR

1 TEASPOON SALT

2 EGGS

2 TABLESPOONS OLIVE OIL

100 g (3½ oz) ZIBBIBO
RAISINS OR SMALL
SEEDLESS MUSCATELS

4 TABLESPOONS
CHOPPED ROSEMARY

———

*Makes 9 panini or
1 big loaf*

These are flavoursome small rolls, full of raisins and rosemary. They are typical of Florence and are great simply plain as a snack (or merenda, as they say in Italy). I also like them toasted with a nice mature pecorino or goat's cheese. Toasted and spread with butter and jam is delicious, too.

Crumble the yeast into a large bowl. Add the honey, water and a large handful of flour. Whisk until smooth, then set aside until the yeast begins to activate. Add the rest of the flour, the salt and 1 of the eggs, whisked lightly. Mix until a dough forms, then knead with floured hands on a lightly floured surface until smooth and compact, adding a little more flour or water if necessary. Return to the bowl, mark a cross in the top and cover with a tea towel. Leave in a warm place for about an hour to puff up.

Put the olive oil and raisins in a small saucepan. Gently sauté until the raisins have absorbed most of the oil, have plumped up and are a bit golden. Add the rosemary, along with 6 or 7 good grinds of black pepper and stir until it is heated through and smells good. Remove from the heat and leave to cool.

When the dough has risen remove it to a lightly floured work surface. Add the raisin mixture and knead until incorporated. Divide the dough into 9 portions and shape each into a smooth round ball. If you prefer, you can leave it as 1 large loaf. Put on a baking tray lined with baking paper, with space in between for spreading, and leave to rise, covered, for 35–40 minutes.

Preheat the oven to 180°C (350°F/Gas 4). Whisk the remaining egg and brush gently over the top of each ball of dough, then scatter a little fine salt over them. Bake for 20–25 minutes, until golden on the top and bottom. (A large loaf may need up to 10 minutes longer in the oven.) The rolls can be frozen once cooled completely.

Capitolo
- C H A P T E R -

SNACK

BOX

GRILLED SEPPIE & ZUCCHINI

NEW GARLIC OMELETTE

OMELETTE WITH BLOSSOMS

FRIED ACACIA BLOSSOMS

CROSTINI WITH ANCHOVY,
SEMI-DRIED TOMATO & MASCARPONE

MARISA'S PUMPKIN CROSTONE

TOMATO, MOZZARELLA
& HERB BRUSCHETTA

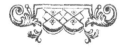

No. 322. 1s.

The

SNACK

BOX

THE SMALL THINGS

Isn't it lovely how the
casalinga Italiana has
such a knack ...

TO SPREAD OUT A MEAL
SO SMOOTHLY AND SO FLUENTLY.
TO TURN OUT AN ANTIPASTO
– A NIBBLE HERE AND THERE.
TO SLIP IN AN EXTRA LAYER WITH
BITS AND PIECES TAKEN FROM
THIS AND THAT. A SMALL CROSTINO,
AN EGG, A FEW SLIVERS OF
BUTTER AND ANCHOVIES ...
TO MAKE PEOPLE HAPPY.

GRILLED SEPPIE & ZUCCHINI

400 g (14 oz) SMALL TO MEDIUM
SEPPIE (CUTTLEFISH)

2 WHOLE GARLIC
CLOVES, PEELED

4 TABLESPOONS OLIVE OIL

JUICE OF 1 LEMON

PINCH OF GROUND CHILLI

1 TEASPOON DRIED OREGANO

400 g (14 oz/ABOUT 3)
ZUCCHINI (COURGETTES), CUT
DIAGONALLY INTO ROUNDS
OF 3–4 cm (1¼–1½ inches)

1 TABLESPOON
CHOPPED PARSLEY

SMALL FISTFUL OF
BASIL LEAVES

Serves 6 as an antipasto

This is a lovely antipasto that could be followed by a whole grilled or roasted fish, for example. On the other hand it could also make a light summer lunch on its own. It's great warm, but also good at room temperature.

Clean the seppie. Remove the ink sac, cut off the wings and keep aside, then remove the beaky part around the tentacles and discard. Pull out and discard the quill. Leave the tentacles whole, or halve if big. Open out the body and slash it on the inside (not all the way through) so it won't curl horizontally during cooking.

Squash a garlic clove with a large knife and combine with 2 tablespoons of olive oil, the lemon juice and chilli. Crumble in the oregano and season with salt and pepper.

Heat the remaining 2 tablespoons of olive oil in a large non-stick frying pan, add the other whole garlic clove and the zucchini and sauté until the zucchini is nicely coloured and cooked through, but not soggy. Toss the pan now and then to turn the zucchini. Season with salt and pepper.

Put a chargrill pan over high heat and when it's very hot add the cuttlefish steaks, and the tentacles and wings on the sides. Cook until they turn opaque and golden marks appear underneath, then turn and cook the other side. Remove to a board and scatter with a little salt. Slice up the steaks and tentacles into strips of about 5 mm (¼ inch). Arrange the zucchini on your serving plate and then layer the cuttlefish on top. Scatter with the parsley and tear the basil over. Drizzle on the dressing. Give a final grind or two of black pepper. Serve immediately or leave for a while for the flavours to mingle. Serve with bread.

SAPIENTE
WORDS/PAROLE

YOU CAN'T MAKE AN OMELETTE
WITHOUT BREAKING THE EGGS

**20 g (¾ oz) OR SO RINSED,
ROUGHLY SLICED NEW GARLIC,
WHITE WITH SOME GREEN**

1 TABLESPOON OLIVE OIL

1 EGG

Serves 1

NEW GARLIC OMELETTE

*Nonna said she went to see a woman in the countryside
who asked her at the last minute to stay to lunch. She
then dashed into her field to collect some new garlic in its
brief season. Nonna said it was the best omelette she'd
tasted, yet with almost nothing in it — just the contadina's
eggs and garlic. You just need a piece of bread on the
side and you can add parmesan to serve, if you like.
It is lovely, simple and pure.*

In a small non-stick frying pan of about 13 cm (5 inches)
that has a lid, sauté the garlic very gently in the olive oil.
Add just a few grains of salt and stir so it doesn't get dark
in any places but just softens and turns golden. Whip the
egg in a bowl with a dash of salt.

Pour the egg over the evenly distributed garlic and
cook on a strong heat at first, using a wooden spatula to
push down any sides that have swayed up. Turn the heat
right down and cover with a lid, cooking until the omelette
is just set but still a little creamy on top. If you feel it is
getting too dark underneath and the top is not yet set, you
can turn off the heat and leave the lid on for half a minute
or so, but don't leave it too long or it can become rubbery.
It must still be creamy on top. Serve at once with a grind
of pepper and a little extra salt sprinkled over if needed.

HANDFUL OF EDIBLE SMALL
UNSPRAYED FLOWERS OR
PETALS (ACACIA, SAMBUCO/
ELDERFLOWER, VIOLETS, ROSES)

1 EGG

A LITTLE OLIVE OIL

1 TABLESPOON GRATED
PARMESAN, PLUS
EXTRA, TO SERVE

FRESHLY GROUND PINK
PEPPERCORNS, TO SERVE

———

Serves 1

OMELETTE WITH BLOSSOMS

*A lovely springtime dish to add a splash of colour
and health.*

If necessary, rinse the petals very gently and pat them dry.
Halve them if they are big and remove any inner parts.
Whip the egg in a small bowl. Heat a splash of oil in a
13 cm (5 inch) non-stick frying pan that has a lid and swirl
it around so the bottom is covered.

   Pour the egg in, using a wooden spatula to push down
any sides that have swayed up. Turn the heat right down.
Scatter the parmesan over the top and as soon as it starts
to melt, scatter the blossoms over. Cover with a lid for
a few moments to just set them in, so the egg remains
creamy on top. Serve at once with a grind of pink pepper
and extra parmesan if you like.

FRIED ACACIA BLOSSOMS

*When the acacia blossoms appear on the trees you
shouldn't delay, as the season comes and goes very
quickly. This is lovely served with an aperitivo of prosecco
or white wine, or alongside a main course. When fried,
they have a crisp, fresh, slightly sweet taste. Make sure the
acacia blossoms you get are the edible type, as they can
vary from place to place.*

Collect sprigs of acacia when the flowers are plump and
fresh, not drying out on their branches. Make up a loose
batter with an egg, flour, a little milk and a pinch of salt.
Dip the flowers in the batter, letting the excess drip away.

   Heat some light olive oil in a frying pan. Fry the slim
branches until golden, then drain on paper towels. Serve
hot and strip away at the fried flowers with your teeth.

CROSTINI WITH ANCHOVY, SEMI-DRIED TOMATO & MASCARPONE

30 g (1 oz) RED ONION, SLICED

SPLASH OF RED WINE VINEGAR

30 g (1 oz) SEMI-DRIED
TOMATOES

3 TABLESPOONS OLIVE OIL

8 ANCHOVY FILLETS,
CHOPPED COARSELY

1 TABLESPOON
CHOPPED PARSLEY

1 TEASPOON FINELY
CHOPPED ROSEMARY

5 SLICES COUNTRY-STYLE
BREAD, ROUGHLY 6 cm
(2½ inches) IN DIAMETER

ABOUT 3 TABLESPOONS
MASCARPONE

Makes 5

I love starting a meal with a small bite of something interesting, such as this. Italians always do this sort of thing well and it takes the meal to a different level. It's quite possible that you will have all the ingredients at home already, apart from the mascarpone perhaps.

Soak the onion in cold water with the splash of vinegar for 20 minutes or so. At the same time, soak the semi-dried tomatoes in warm water to plump them up.

Drain the tomatoes and chop them into quite large, long pieces. Put them in a bowl with the olive oil. Drain the onion and add to the bowl, along with the anchovies, parsley, rosemary and a few grinds of black pepper. Grill the bread. Roughly spread a couple of teaspoons of mascarpone over each crostino, then top with the anchovy mixture and serve.

MARISA'S PUMPKIN CROSTONE

THE
LIST

1 kg (2 lb 4 oz) PUMPKIN
(WINTER SQUASH)

3 TABLESPOONS OLIVE OIL,
PLUS EXTRA, FOR DRIZZLING

100 g (3½ oz) WHITE
ONION, CHOPPED

10–12 SAGE LEAVES

250 ml (9 fl oz/1 cup) WATER

6 SLICES COUNTRY-STYLE BREAD

1 WHOLE GARLIC CLOVE, PEELED

3 TABLESPOONS BUTTER

6 TABLESPOONS
GRATED PARMESAN

Makes 6

This is lovely and really easy as a starter. And such a simple way to slide an extra vegetable into a meal.

Peel the pumpkin, remove the seeds and cut it into large chunks. Heat the olive oil in a large saucepan and sauté the onion until pale golden and soft. Add a couple of the sage leaves and cook for a minute to flavour, then add the pumpkin, water and some salt and pepper. Put the lid on and simmer for 30–40 minutes, until the pumpkin has collapsed. Check now and then that nothing is sticking or it doesn't need a few more drops of water. Taste for salt.

Grill the bread. Lightly rub one side of each piece with garlic and drizzle a little olive oil over. Top with a good heap of warm pumpkin. Put the remaining sage leaves and the butter in a small saucepan and heat until the sage is crisp and the butter is golden. If the butter is getting too dark before the sage is crisp, add a little more to the pan. Drizzle the butter over the pumpkin, scatter the parmesan and crisp sage leaves on top and give a good grind of black pepper. Serve hot.

SAPIENTE

WORDS/PAROLE

TOMATO, MOZZARELLA & HERB BRUSCHETTA

THE
LIST

2 SLICES
COUNTRY-STYLE
BREAD

1 WHOLE GARLIC CLOVE,
PEELED

ABOUT 4 TABLESPOONS
OLIVE OIL

4 THICK LARGE SLICES
OF TOMATO

½ TABLESPOON
CHOPPED OREGANO

4 x 1 cm (½ inch)
THICK SLICES FRESH
MOZZARELLA

SMALL FISTFUL OF
BASIL LEAVES

Serves 2

Simplicity. This is a quick pizza really, a delicious snack that you can throw together in a moment.

Preheat the oven to 220°C (425°F/Gas 7).

Toast the bread directly on the oven rack until both sides are just lightly golden. Rub garlic over one side of each slice, then put on a baking tray and drizzle 1 tablespoon of olive oil over each. Cover each with 2 slices of tomato, then a little drizzle of oil and season with salt and a few grinds of pepper. Scatter some of the oregano over, then top with the mozzarella slices and the rest of the oregano. Put in the oven and cook until the mozzarella starts to melt. Put on plates, give a final drizzle of olive oil and scatter over the basil leaves. Give one or two grinds of black pepper and serve at once.

– THE –

Vegetable Patch

ARTICHOKE & MINT SOUP

TOMATO SOUP WITH RICE & BASIL

AUTUMN VEGETABLE SOUP

VEGETABLES WITH 'BAGNA CAUDA'

RADICCHIO & APPLE SALAD

GREEN SALAD

MARTA'S MUM'S FENNEL

MARISA'S POTATOES WITH CRUMBS

SAUTEED ARTICHOKES
& POTATOES

SALT & PEPPER POTATOES WITH
A TRICKLE OF BUTTERMILK

SALT & BALSAMIC VINEGAR
SAUTEED POTATOES

SAUTEED CARDOONS
WITH PARMESAN

ZUCCHINI & FLOWERS

MARIELLA'S ZUCCHINI

No
5

WE ASKED FOR CAVOLO NERO AT THE
MARKET AND THE *FRUTTIVENDOLO* SAID
TO COME BACK – WHEN WE HAD OUR
WARM WINTER COATS ON, THEN THE
CAVOLO NERO WOULD BE READY

ARTICHOKE & MINT SOUP

THE
LIST

400 g (14 oz) POTATOES, PEELED
AND CUT INTO CHUNKS

1 ONION, ROUGHLY CHOPPED

1 SMALL CELERY STICK,
CUT INTO CHUNKS

1 SMALL CARROT, PEELED
AND CUT INTO CHUNKS

1.5 litres (52 fl oz/6 cups)
WATER, APPROXIMATELY

2 TABLESPOONS OLIVE OIL,
PLUS EXTRA, TO SERVE

4 ARTICHOKES, WITH ABOUT
12 cm (4½ inches) OF STEM

GRATED PARMESAN, TO SERVE

HANDFUL OF MINT
LEAVES, TO SERVE

Serves 6

This is a good and healthy bowlful of soup for a primo. Be sure to include some of the artichoke stems as they too are rich in iron. Have a bowl of water with some lemon squeezed in on the side to keep the outer artichoke leaves that you strip away and would otherwise discard. (Later you can dip the tender bottoms of these leaves in olive oil and a little salt as a snack.) I like to serve this soup with small squares of bread fried in olive oil until golden.

Put the potatoes, onion, celery, carrot, water and olive oil in a large pot. Season with salt and bring to the boil.

Meanwhile, clean the artichokes. Cut off the stems and strip away the outer woody part of each until you reach the paler tender part. Chop these up and put in the pot. Now, strip away the outer leaves from the artichokes until you reach the more tender inner ones, then cut off and discard the top third of each. Now is a good time to taste a leaf and check you've gone far enough in to be able to eat the whole leaf without having any fibrous bits left in your mouth. Cut the artichokes in half, then cut out and discard the hairy choke. Give the artichokes a quick rinse and then chop up in large chunks directly into the pot.

Cover and simmer for 30 minutes or until the vegetables are tender. Using a hand-held blender, purée until completely smooth. Check that the consistency is good, adding a little hot water if it seems too thick. Taste for salt. Serve hot, with an extra drizzle of olive oil, some grated parmesan, a few grinds of black pepper and the mint leaves torn over each bowl.

4 TABLESPOONS OLIVE OIL,
PLUS EXTRA, FOR SERVING

1 SMALL RED ONION, CHOPPED

2 GARLIC CLOVES, CHOPPED

800 g (1 lb 12 oz) VERY
RIPE TOMATOES, PEELED
AND CHOPPED

12–15 BASIL LEAVES

1.25 litres (44 fl oz/5 cups)
HOT WATER

180 g (6¼ oz) SHORT-GRAIN
WHITE RICE

6–8 TABLESPOONS GRATED
PARMESAN, TO SERVE

Serves 5 or 6

TOMATO SOUP WITH RICE & BASIL

This is simple and summery, just the thing for when you have beautiful ripe tomatoes in your vegetable patch. How can it not be great, with tomatoes, basil, olive oil and garlic?

Heat the olive oil in a large pot and sauté the onion until nicely golden and a bit sticky. Add the garlic and when it smells great, add the tomatoes. Bring to the boil and season with salt and pepper. Tear in about 7 of the basil leaves and simmer for 5 minutes or so, squashing down most of the tomato lumps with a potato masher. Add the hot water and simmer, covered, for about 20 minutes.

Add the rice and simmer for another 20 minutes or so, putting the lid on at the end to prevent too much liquid evaporating. It should be quite thick, but if it seems too thick just add a little hot water. Taste for seasoning and adjust if necessary.

Serve in wide bowls. Tear a couple of basil leaves in half and add to each bowl. Scatter a heaped tablespoon or so of parmesan over each and drizzle with a little olive oil. Grind a little black pepper over and serve.

AUTUMN VEGETABLE SOUP

250 g (9 oz/1¼ cups) BORLOTTI
(CRANBERRY) BEANS,
SOAKED IN PLENTY OF
COLD WATER OVERNIGHT

5 GARLIC CLOVES,
PEELED, 3 CHOPPED

A FEW SAGE LEAVES OR
A SMALL CLUMP

300 g (10½ oz) YOUNG
CAVOLO NERO

4 TABLESPOONS EXTRA
VIRGIN OLIVE OIL, PLUS
EXTRA, FOR SERVING

200 g (7 oz) RED
ONIONS, CHOPPED

1 LEEK, TRIMMED, WHITE PART
AND SOME GREEN TOO, SLICED

160 g (5½ oz) INNER
CELERY STICKS WITH SOME
LEAVES, CHOPPED

300 g (10½ oz) CARROTS,
PEELED AND SLICED

400 g (14 oz) POTATOES, PEELED
AND CUT INTO LARGE CHUNKS

300 g (10½ oz) CABBAGE,
TRIMMED AND SHREDDED

2 litres (70 fl oz/8 cups)
WATER

8 SLICES COUNTRY-STYLE BREAD

GROUND CHILLI, TO SERVE

GRATED PARMESAN,
TO SERVE, IF YOU LIKE

Serves 6–8

*This is a huge, warm and friendly pot of everything.
It would be made when the new extra virgin olive oil of the
season is ready and this would be used during the cooking
and also drizzled over the soup just before serving. You
need a big pot, of course. You can vary the vegetables,
but whatever you use should be cut up irregularly so
they're all different, rather than an army of the same.
I like to cook the borlotti beans in a pressure cooker.*

Drain the water from the borlotti beans after soaking
overnight. Put the beans in a pot, cover with plenty of fresh
water and add a whole clove of garlic and the sage leaves.
Bring to the boil, cover and simmer over low heat for
1 hour or as long as necessary, until the beans are tender.
Check now and then that there is an abundant amount of
water covering the beans. Add salt only towards the end
of the cooking time. Take off the heat, but don't drain.

To prepare the cavolo nero, hold each stalk at its base
and use your other hand to strip the leaf off. Shred the
leaves and discard the stalks.

Meanwhile, heat the olive oil in a large wide pot and
sauté the onions and leek until lightly golden. Add the
chopped garlic and sauté for a moment. Add the celery
and carrots and sauté for a while longer. Turn through with
a wooden spoon. Add the potatoes, cabbage and cavolo
nero, season with salt and a little pepper and add 1.5 litres
(52 fl oz/6 cups) of the water. Bring to the boil, then lower
the heat and simmer, partly covered, until the vegetables
are lovely and tender, about 1 hour 15 minutes. Add the
remaining 500 ml (17 fl oz/2 cups) of water as the soup
thickens, about halfway through the cooking time.

Drain the borlotti beans, keeping the cooking broth.
Purée 1 cup of the beans with 500 ml of the broth. Add
to the pot with the whole beans and simmer for another
15 minutes or so to blend all of the flavours. If it seems too
tight, add a little more of the borlotti broth. Remove from
the heat and rest, covered.

Grill the bread. Rub one side gently with the remaining
garlic clove, then drizzle a little olive oil over each slice.
Ladle the soup into bowls and top each with a good
dribble of olive oil, a grind of pepper and a scattering
of chilli. You can decide whether you would like this with
grated parmesan or without.

VEGETABLES WITH 'BAGNA CAUDA'

◇◇

150 g (5½ oz) ANCHOVIES IN SALT

375 ml (13 fl oz/1½ cups)
MILK

ABOUT 10 GARLIC CLOVES,
COARSELY CHOPPED

7 TABLESPOONS OLIVE OIL,
PLUS A LITTLE EXTRA

PINCH OF GROUND CHILLI

YOUR CHOICE OF VEGETABLES

HARD-BOILED EGGS

TOASTED SLICES OF
COUNTRY-STYLE BREAD

ROSEMARY LEAVES

Serves 4

This can stand alone as a main meal, but would also be good before a grilled fish dish. It is from northern Italy, where the sauce is traditionally kept warm over a flame so the vegetables can be dipped in it as everybody talks the night away. Here I have made a sauce to serve with a platter of vegetables. You can use any vegetables of your choice. The kind of anchovies to use are those whole ones packed in salt that usually come in beautiful huge tins.

Rinse the anchovies and fillet them, removing the central bone. Put in a bowl and cover with 125 ml (4 fl oz/½ cup) of milk. Leave to soak for half an hour or so. Meanwhile, in a medium saucepan sauté the garlic in 4 tablespoons of olive oil until it smells good. Add the remaining milk and simmer, partly covered and stirring regularly so the garlic doesn't stick, for 20 minutes or so, until pulpy.

When the garlic is very soft mash it into the milk in the saucepan with a potato masher or fork until puréed. Drain the anchovies, discarding the milk, then pat dry with paper towels and chop them up finely. Add to the garlic purée in the saucepan, along with the remaining 3 tablespoons of olive oil and a good grinding of black pepper. Simmer, stirring very regularly, for about 10 minutes. Remove from the heat and stir in the chilli and extra olive oil, if needed.

Prepare your accompaniments while the sauce is cooking. For example, boil potatoes in salted water, blanch cauliflower florets, hard-boil a couple of eggs. Rinse and trim spring onions (scallions), carrots, inner celery sticks with some leaves, fennel, red peppers (capsicums), artichokes. Rinse tomatoes, radishes, green radicchio leaves. Grill a few slices of bread. Chop enough rosemary leaves to fill a small plate. Arrange them all on platters or suitable serving dishes and serve with the sauce, which must be served warm with an extra grind of black pepper.

RADICCHIO
& APPLE SALAD

20 g (¾ oz) SMALL RED BULB
SPRING ONION (SCALLION)

SPLASH OF WINE VINEGAR

½ RED APPLE (I LIKE THE FUJI
VARIETY HERE), UNPEELED

1–2 TEASPOONS FRESHLY
SQUEEZED LEMON JUICE

80 g (2¾ oz) RED
RADICCHIO LEAVES

6 WALNUT HALVES

1 TEASPOON CHESTNUT HONEY

3 TABLESPOONS OLIVE OIL

1 TABLESPOON
BALSAMIC VINEGAR

ABOUT 40 g (1½ oz) SHAVED
MATURE PECORINO
OR PARMESAN

Serves 2

I love a salad like this — full of colour, crunch and flavour, yet so simple to put together. It has a rather strong autumnal feel. This is about strewing good ingredients onto a plate and reaping the benefits in the overall flavour and freshness.

Thinly slice the onion and put in a small bowl of cold water with the vinegar (this helps to get rid of the acidity in the onion). Leave to soak for 20 minutes or so. Cut the apple into 2–3 mm (1/16–1/8 inch) slices and put in a bowl of cold water with the lemon juice and a sprinkling of salt.

Cut away the thick white spine from the radicchio, then tear up or shred the leaves thickly. Divide between 2 plates and arrange in a nice heap. Shake the apple dry and arrange in and around the radicchio. Scatter a little salt over, then break up the walnuts with your fingers and scatter on top. Drain and rinse the onion, pat dry with paper towel and scatter over the salad.

For the dressing, put the honey in a small bowl and stir in the olive oil and balsamic vinegar with a little salt and pepper. Mix with a small whisk or fork to dissolve the honey, then drizzle over the salads. Scatter the pecorino on top, give a few grinds of black pepper and serve.

SAPIENTE
WORDS/PAROLE

A HALVED ONION IS GOOD FOR CLEANING GOLD AND SILVER GILDED FRAMES, AND MAKING THEM SHINE

80 g (2¾ oz)
TRIMMED SPRING
ONION (SCALLION) WITH
SOME GREEN PART

80 g (2¾ oz) INNER CELERY
STICKS WITH LEAVES

80 g (2¾ oz) CUCUMBER, PEELED

40 g (1½ oz) VALERIANA
(LAMB'S LETTUCE)

40 g (1½ oz) RUCOLA
(ARUGULA)

2 TABLESPOONS VERY
COARSELY CHOPPED PARSLEY

1 TABLESPOON OLIVE OIL

JUICE OF 1 SMALL LEMON

½ FULLY RIPE AVOCADO

SMALL HANDFUL OF
MINT LEAVES

Serves 4

GREEN SALAD

*I love this salad next to anything, even my bed!
I could eat it all day and never be tired, ever. It refreshes
and recharges me. If your rucola is large, tear it in half.
I only use a little oil as the lemon carries this salad along
and the avocado holds the richness. Needless to say,
your avocado must be a beauty — at full ripeness, but not
past this. It can make or break the situation. If valeriana
is unavailable, you could use picked watercress leaves.*

Rinse, dry and chop the spring onion, celery and
cucumber and put in a bowl with the valeriana, rucola
and parsley. Add a little salt and pepper. Mix the oil and
lemon juice together in a small bowl or cup with a little salt
and pepper. Pour over the salad and mix through gently.
Scoop chunks of avocado into the salad, tear the mint
leaves in, gently turn through again and serve soon.

3 FENNEL BULBS, TRIMMED

5 TABLESPOONS OLIVE OIL

2 WHOLE GARLIC
CLOVES, PEELED

400 g (14 oz) TIN
CHOPPED TOMATOES

4 BASIL LEAVES

ABOUT 3 TABLESPOONS FLOUR

1 TABLESPOON DRY
BREADCRUMBS

2 TABLESPOONS
GRATED PARMESAN

Serves 6

MARTA'S MUM'S FENNEL

This is from my friend Marta's mother. It's a wonderful way with fennel. She says that it is important to cook it for a long time so the fennel is given time to dry, to get it beyond the waterlogged aspect it can sometimes have. I use an oval ceramic dish to make these in, where the fennel fits compactly in a single layer. It is lovely with fish and meat, particularly pork.

Quarter the fennel bulbs from the top down, making sure the pieces stay hinged together. Bring a pot of salted water to the boil and cook the fennel for 10 minutes or so, until softened but not soggy and overdone. Test with a fork to see that it is tender. Drain in a colander and pat dry with paper towels.

Preheat the oven to 180°C (350°F/Gas 4).

Heat 2 tablespoons of the oil with 1 garlic clove in a small pot until it smells good. Add the tomatoes with some salt and pepper, and simmer for 10 minutes or so, until it is a sauce. Tear in the basil just towards the end so it will perfume the tomato. Remove from the heat.

Use a large non-stick frying pan for the fennel. Put the flour in a bowl and pat it onto the fennel, coating it on all sides. Heat the remaining 3 tablespoons of olive oil in the pan. Add the fennel, in one layer, and the other garlic clove. Saute the fennel until golden and firm on all sides. If the garlic browns, remove it as it will have done its job.

Dollop about half the tomato sauce here and there on the bottom of the oven dish that you'll bake the fennel in. Arrange the fennel in so it all fits compactly. If some of the pieces are very big, halve them. Dollop the rest of the tomato sauce on top. Scatter the breadcrumbs and parmesan over and bake for about 20 minutes or until the top is golden and crusty in places. Serve warm. Also lovely at room temperature.

si facевo sempre [...]

fece accostiare [...]

e lo baccio or rod [...]

suoi suoi petah [...]

Ed egli murì a[...]

uore qualche co[...]

ribиare tutto su[...]

fibre vellutate [...]

Pass - ribu[...]

povero sogno dor[...]

spengеto con [...]

...u odari, per ...
...talmente il ...
...et una pioggia ...
...ellutati ......
...re in boccia, nuovo...
...di grande di al...
...no amore che tene...
...i suoi petali ro...
...coli per l'ultima ...
...bella, e rovine dolo...
...una bufera strana...

MARISA'S POTATOES WITH CRUMBS

ABOUT 1.2 kg (2 lb 10 oz)
POTATOES

7 TABLESPOONS OLIVE OIL

2 FISTFULS OF DRY
BREADCRUMBS

12 BIG SAGE LEAVES

Serves 6 or more

Everybody loves Nonna Marisa's potatoes. Marisa is always making brodo and sugo and distributing them among her kin, in between doing their ironing and loving her grandchildren. It is important to use a non-stick baking dish for this.

Preheat the oven to 200°C (400°F/Gas 6). Peel the potatoes and cut into chunks, not too big. Keep in a bowl of cold water until you are ready to cook them.

Pour half the olive oil onto the bottom of a non-stick baking dish, about 22 x 30 cm (8½ x 12 inches). Pour the potatoes into a colander and immediately scatter the breadcrumbs over so they'll stick to the clinging water. Turn through once with your hands, then tip the potatoes and crumbs into the baking dish. Scatter with the sage leaves (torn in half if very big), and salt and pepper. Add the rest of the olive oil and toss through quickly but thoroughly, making sure each potato is well coated.

Roast the potatoes for about 50 minutes, turning only after the bottoms are golden, about 35 minutes. Turn again until crusty and golden all over. Taste to check they have enough salt, then serve at once.

SAUTEED ARTICHOKES
& POTATOES

5 ARTICHOKES, WITH ABOUT
6 cm (2½ inches) STEM ATTACHED

JUICE OF 1 LEMON

4 TABLESPOONS OLIVE OIL

2 SPRING ONIONS (SCALLIONS),
TRIMMED AND CHOPPED

400 g (14 oz) POTATOES, PEELED,
HALVED AND SLICED INTO
3–4 mm (⅛ inch) ROUNDS

2 GARLIC CLOVES, CHOPPED

60 ml (2 fl oz/¼ cup) WATER

1 TEASPOON DRIED OREGANO

1 TABLESPOON
CHOPPED PARSLEY

Serves 4–6

Trim away the outer dark-green part of the artichoke stems to get to the paler inner part. Tear away the tough outer leaves to get to the tender inner ones that will not be fibrous in your mouth when cooked. Cut off the top third of the artichokes, then halve them lengthways. Scoop out the hairy chokes with a small knife or teaspoon. Cut each half into 4 lengths, still attached at the stem. Put in a bowl of water with the lemon juice squeezed in and leave until you are ready for them.

Heat the oil in a wide non-stick frying pan. Add the spring onions and sauté a bit before adding the potatoes and drained artichokes. Sauté gently until a little golden here and there. Add the garlic and some salt and pepper and sauté a little more. Add the water and simmer, uncovered, for about 20 minutes or until all are tender. Add the oregano and parsley and continue cooking until almost all the pan juices have been absorbed. Taste for seasoning, then serve.

SALT & PEPPER POTATOES WITH A TRICKLE OF BUTTERMILK

6–8 MEDIUM POTATOES

ABOUT 8 TEASPOONS
PEPPER SALT (PAGE 25), PLUS
A LITTLE EXTRA, TO SERVE

ABOUT 150 g (5½ oz) BUTTER

ABOUT 375 ml (13 fl oz/
1½ cups) BUTTERMILK

Serves 6–8

There's not much to this — just whole potatoes, scattered with a crunchy salt and pepper mix, then baked in foil. A blob of butter and a little buttermilk makes them soft and creamy. They are simple and so very good, especially with roasted meats. Have the butter and buttermilk at room temperature so they don't cool down the potatoes.

Preheat the oven to 200°C (400°F/Gas 6). Tear pieces of foil, each large enough to wrap a potato in, and put in a pile. Wash the potatoes well and scrub the skins. Hold each potato over a piece of foil, prick it here and there with a fork, and while still damp (so it sticks) scatter over a heaped teaspoon of the pepper salt. The amount you need will depend on the size of the potatoes.

Wrap up each potato in foil and put on a baking tray. Bake for about 50 minutes or until the potatoes surrender easily when pressed. Remove from the oven. Take a little extra pepper salt, and crush it a little finer to serve on the side. Serve the potatoes hot and still in the foil, for everyone to unwrap their own. They should be halved down the middle, pressed up from the bottom to fluff up, then topped with a blob of butter and a good trickle of buttermilk. Sprinkle the crushed pepper salt over the top.

SALT & BALSAMIC VINEGAR SAUTEED POTATOES

THE
----- LIST -----

SOME COARSE SALT

1 kg (2 lb 4 oz) POTATOES

4 TABLESPOONS OLIVE OIL

2 WHOLE GARLIC
CLOVES, PEELED

125 ml (4 fl oz/½ cup)
BALSAMIC VINEGAR

2 BRANCHES ROSEMARY, PLUS
EXTRA, TO SERVE (OPTIONAL)

Serves 6

These are easy to make and go well with a plain roasted meat. It's good to make a stovetop potato dish when your oven is full of roasting meat.

In a mortar, crush some coarse salt with a pestle to break it down a bit, but still leave some texture. Peel the potatoes, rinse them, halve lengthways and cut into gondolas. Heat the olive oil in a large non-stick frying pan that has a lid. Add the potatoes and garlic cloves and sauté on a fairly high heat, turning through and tossing until they have a bit of colour and are starting to stick. Season with some of the crushed salt and a little pepper. Add half the vinegar and turn through. Sit the rosemary branches on top, cover with a lid and lower the heat.

Simmer for about 15 minutes or so, until the potatoes are tender and much of the vinegar seems to have been absorbed. Add the rest of the vinegar, turn through and cook, uncovered now, for 10 minutes or until the potatoes are tender and crisping up just a bit and most of the liquid has reduced. Sprinkle a little extra salt on and serve hot with a couple of extra rosemary branches on top if you like. These are also surprisingly good at room temperature.

2 LEMONS

1.2 kg (2 lb 10 oz) CARDOONS

4 TABLESPOONS OLIVE OIL

2 WHOLE GARLIC
CLOVES, PEELED

GOOD PINCH OF GROUND CHILLI

6 TABLESPOONS
GRATED PARMESAN

Serves 4–6

SAUTEED CARDOONS WITH PARMESAN

I like to serve this elegant dish with roast guinea fowl or lamb. The cardoons have a bitter, yet beautiful flavour that stays with you. The work involved in stripping and cleaning them is well worth it. Wilma says that when boiling cardoons one can put a clean tea towel over them in the water to make sure they are all immersed. Cardoons, like artichokes, are very good for you. If cardoons are not available, you could use thistles instead.

Have a bowl of cold water ready with the juice of 1 lemon squeezed in. If the cardoons are attached, separate the sticks from the base. Leave the tender very inner sticks whole with their leaves attached (cook them with the rest, then eat them with some oil and lemon juice). Wearing gloves and using a small sharp knife or potato peeler, strip away the outer strings of the sticks by digging in at one end of the stick and dragging all the way down. The strings are unpleasant to eat so make sure you get all of them. As you work, cut the sticks into irregular lengths of 6 or 7 cm (2½ or 2¾ inches) and drop them into the lemon water so they don't darken. Make sure they are submerged.

Bring a pot of salted water to the boil. Add the drained cardoons and squeeze in the juice of the remaining lemon. Boil, uncovered, for about 35 minutes or until the cardoons are tender when poked with a fork. You may need to remove the thinner sticks if they are cooked before the rest are ready. Drain well.

Heat the oil in a large non-stick frying pan and add the cardoons, garlic, chilli and salt and pepper. Sauté until golden here and there, about 15 minutes or longer if necessary. Remove from the heat, scatter the parmesan over the top and put the lid on for a few minutes so the cheese melts into the cardoons. Serve warm.

750 g (1 lb 10 oz/ABOUT 7)
ZUCCHINI (COURGETTES),
WITH FLOWERS ATTACHED

10 OR SO ZUCCHINI
FLOWERS, EXTRA

1 SMALL RED ONION, CHOPPED

4 TABLESPOONS OLIVE OIL

2 GARLIC CLOVES, CHOPPED

400 g (14 oz) TIN
CHOPPED TOMATOES

ABOUT 125 ml (4 fl oz/
½ cup) WATER

FISTFUL OF BASIL
LEAVES, TORN

Serves 6

ZUCCHINI & FLOWERS

This is a great two-in-one recipe. The dark-green outer part of the zucchini is stripped off and can be served as part of an antipasto (see below) or with a main course. Use zucchini that aren't too big in diameter.

Remove the flowers attached to the zucchini and put with the extra flowers. Rinse the zucchini. Peel away the dark-green outer part in long strips (use in the recipe below). Slice the zucchini into 1.5 cm (5⁄8 inch) slices. Sauté the onion in the oil in a wide pan until golden and cooked, then add the garlic. Sauté for a moment and when it smells good, add the tomatoes. Turn through and cook for a few minutes before adding the zucchini slices. Season with salt and pepper and add the water, which you can first swish around in the tomato tin. Cover and simmer for 20 minutes or so, until the zucchini is tender.

Meanwhile, open up the zucchini flowers and remove all the inner parts, discarding those. Rinse the flowers gently and pat dry with paper towels. Shred each into 2 or 3 pieces. Add the flowers and basil to the pan, turn through, and continue cooking, covered, for 10 minutes or so. If the sauce looks too tight, add a few drops of hot water but it is a side dish, not a soup! Remove from the heat and leave with the lid on for 10 minutes or so, or until you serve them. These are also nice at room temperature.

ZUCCHINI (COURGETTE)
STRIPS (SEE ABOVE)

3 TABLESPOONS OLIVE OIL

½ TEASPOON FINELY
GRATED LEMON RIND,
YELLOW PART ONLY

JUICE OF ½ LEMON

SMALL HANDFUL OF MINT LEAVES

Serves 4–6

MARIELLA'S ZUCCHINI

Mariella, a wonderful housewife and cook, taught me this. It's easy and such a good idea for using zucchini in a different way.

Put the zucchini strips in a bowl with the oil, lemon rind and juice, salt and pepper. Tear in the mint and turn through to combine. Cover and put in the fridge for an hour or so before serving. Lovely even the next day.

The Pasta Pot

POTATO & TRUFFLE PURSES

RAVIOLI WITH ASPARAGUS, RICOTTA,
SAGE & BROWN BUTTER

BARBARA'S ASPARAGUS & HAM LASAGNA

PASTA AL FORNO SICILIANA

PENNE WITH CALAMARI, ZUCCHINI
& THEIR FLOWERS

SPAGHETTI WITH LENTIL RAGU

RAGU WITH MILK & GREEN TAGLIATELLE

GREEN TAGLIATELLE

SPAGHETTI WITH PANCETTA, PECORINO
& ROSEMARY CRUMBS

SPAGHETTI AGLIO, OLIO, PEPERONCINO
& AVOCADO

GIOVANNA'S SPAGHETTI

SPAGHETTI WITH CLAMS, TOMATO
& A DASH OF CREAM

SPAGHETTI WITH CLAMS & TABASCO

TORTA DI SPAGHETTI

BARBARA'S MUM'S SPINACH POLPETTINE

RISOTTO WITH PRAWNS,
LAVENDER & LEMON

RISOTTO WITH PEARS & PECORINO

QUICK VEGETABLE BROTH

The HOUSE Rules

USE LARGE WIDE PASTA BOWLS THAT YOU CAN TURN THE
PASTA AROUND IN AND, IF POSSIBLE, HAVE THEM WARM

DO NOT PUT THE PASTA ON TO BOIL UNTIL ALL
THE DINERS HAVE ARRIVED

PEOPLE SHOULD COME IMMEDIATELY WHEN THE COOK
CALLS, AS CLOGGING PASTA IS UNACCEPTABLE

ABOUT 2 TEASPOONS OF SALT SHOULD BE ADDED FOR
2.5 LITRES (87 FL OZ/10 CUPS) OF WATER

KEEP A RULE THAT YOU ALWAYS FOLLOW AS TO WHEN
YOU ADD THE SALT TO AVOID NO SALT IN THE PASTA
OR TWICE-SALTED PASTA

REGOLE

PASTA

200 g (7 oz/1⅓ cups) PLAIN
(ALL-PURPOSE) FLOUR

2 EGGS, LIGHTLY BEATEN

1 TEASPOON OLIVE OIL

1 TEASPOON SALT

FILLING

500 g (1 lb 2 oz) POTATOES

2 TABLESPOONS
GRATED PARMESAN

ABOUT 1 TABLESPOON
TRUFFLE BUTTER (PAGE 19)

TO SERVE

2 OUTER LEEK JACKETS,
ABOUT 36 cm
(14¼ inches) LONG

ABOUT 200 g (7 oz)
BUTTER

A WHITE TRUFFLE

GRATED PARMESAN, TO SERVE

Serves 6

POTATO & TRUFFLE PURSES

I like to use white truffles here. The purses are not hard to make, just a bit time-consuming. You will need a pasta machine to roll out the pasta. You'll also need long thin ribbons of leek to hold the purses closed. If you can't get fresh truffle, you can use truffle butter or a few drops of truffle oil. It's worth noting that truffles vary in strength.

To make the pasta, mix the flour, eggs, olive oil and salt in a bowl until the mixture comes together. Turn out and knead well until you have a lovely soft dough. Cover with a tea towel and leave at room temperature to rest for about half an hour or so.

Meanwhile, make the filling. Boil the potatoes in their skins in boiling salted water until soft. At the same time, drop in the leek jackets and boil for a couple of minutes, until tender. Remove, drain and put aside until cool enough to handle. Peel the potatoes while they are still hot by spiking a fork into each and dragging the skin off with a knife using your other hand. Put in a bowl and mash with a potato masher, adding the parmesan, truffle butter and a little salt and pepper if needed. When the leek jackets have cooled, spread them on a board. Standing up so you can see better, cut them into long thin ribbons, a couple of millimetres (fractions of an inch) wide.

Roll out about one–fifth of the dough, keeping the rest covered with a tea towel so it doesn't dry out. Feed the rolled dough through the highest setting on a pasta machine. Fold it up again like a book to neaten it and pass it through this setting again. Now pass it through the next setting twice, and so on until you are 3 notches from the

SAPIENTE
WORDS/PAROLE

TO PREVENT WEEDS GROWING AROUND
POTTED PLANTS, POUR THE WATER
THAT YOU HAVE BOILED POTATOES
WITH SKINS IN OVER THEM. (IT MUST
BE UNSALTED AND COOLED)

finest setting. You can now cut the dough in half to make it more manageable if you like. You want the finished sheet of pasta straight-edged so fold the ends in to straighten, if necessary. Pass through this setting twice, then continue like this until you have used the finest setting and the length of pasta is as wide as the machine allows, with smooth straight edges all around. Proceed with the rest of the dough, keeping the rolled sheets covered with a tea towel so they don't dry out.

Cut the pasta sheets into squares of about 13 cm (5 inches) and keep covered. Working in batches of 5 or so, put about a tablespoon of filling into the middle of a square. Gently draw up the edges to bunch around the filling, being careful not to squash the pasta ruffles. Tie up using a leek ribbon, wrapping it around twice and then tying a knot gently so it doesn't snap. Line up the purses on a tray dusted with a little flour while you finish filling the rest. You will have about 20 purses.

Bring a low-sided wide pot of salted water to the boil. Gently lower some of the purses into the water (don't overcrowd the pot) and simmer for about 5 minutes or until tender. Don't boil rapidly or they may tear. Remove with a slotted spoon to a warm dish while you cook the rest.

Meanwhile, melt the butter to just pale golden. Serve 3 purses per person in warm wide bowls. Drizzle about 2 tablespoons of butter over each bowl, then shave some truffle over the top. Serve at once with a good scattering of parmesan and a grind of pepper.

RAVIOLI WITH ASPARAGUS, RICOTTA, SAGE & BROWN BUTTER

PASTA

200 g (7 oz/1⅓ cups) PLAIN
(ALL-PURPOSE) FLOUR

2 EGGS, LIGHTLY BEATEN

1 TEASPOON OLIVE OIL

1 TEASPOON SALT

400 g (14 oz) ASPARAGUS

3 TABLESPOONS OLIVE OIL

80 g (2¾ oz) SPRING ONIONS
(SCALLIONS) WITH SOME
GREEN PART, CHOPPED

2 TABLESPOONS GRATED
PARMESAN, PLUS EXTRA,
FOR SERVING

250 g (9 oz) FRESH RICOTTA

120 g (4 oz) BUTTER

ABOUT 20 SAGE LEAVES

Serves 6 or more

This is beautiful. And see how easy it is to make a batch of home-made pasta? It's only 2 eggs and 200 g of flour, so you don't need everyone in the family and neighbourhood to help roll it out and your house won't be crammed full of drying pasta.

To make the pasta, mix the flour, eggs, olive oil and salt in a bowl until the mixture comes together. Turn out and knead well until you have a lovely soft dough. Cover with a tea towel and leave at room temperature to rest for about half an hour or so.

Meanwhile, make the filling as it will need time to cool down. Snap off and discard the woody ends of the asparagus. Cut off the tips (about 4 cm/1½ inches) and keep them aside for now. Roughly chop up the rest. Heat the oil in a frying pan and sauté the spring onions until pale gold and softened. Add the chopped asparagus. Sauté, adding a little salt, until tender. Remove to a bowl to cool. When completely cool, add the parmesan and ricotta and mix through well. Taste, adding salt and pepper if needed.

Roll out about one–fifth of the dough, keeping the rest covered with a tea towel so it doesn't dry out. Feed the rolled dough through the highest setting on a pasta machine. Fold it up again like a book to neaten it and pass it through this setting again. Now pass it through the next setting twice, and so on until you are 3 notches from the finest setting. You can now cut the dough in half to make it more manageable if you like. You want the finished sheet of pasta straight-edged so fold the ends in to straighten, if necessary. Pass it through this setting twice, then continue like this until you have used the finest setting and the length of pasta is as wide as the machine allows, with smooth straight edges all around. Proceed with the rest of the dough, keeping the rolled sheets covered with a tea towel so they don't dry out.

Put a pasta sheet on a wooden board. Dollop teaspoons of filling in a row about 3 cm (1¼ inches) in from one long side and with about 3 cm between each. If the pasta is drying out a bit, you may need to brush around the filling with a little water so the two layers of pasta will stick together. Carefully fold the other side over to cover the hills of filling. Press between each one to seal. Cut with a sharp knife between the hills and press firmly with the tines of a fork on the 3 sides that aren't folded. The ravioli should be about 7 x 5 cm (2¾ x 2 inches) but they don't have to be exact. Put them on a lightly floured tray while you make the rest.

Bring a low-sided wide pot of salted water to the boil. Cook the ravioli, in batches, over not-too-high heat for about 5 minutes or until tender. Remove with a slotted spoon to a warm dish while you cook the rest.

While the ravioli are cooking, heat three-quarters of the butter in a pan with the sage leaves and asparagus tips and sauté until the asparagus are a bit golden, the sage is crisp and the butter is golden brown. When the butter starts to brown add the rest to the pan to slow down the process so the sage has time to crisp up. Divide the ravioli among warm plates — 5 per person is a good amount. Divide the asparagus and sage among the plates and spoon some warm butter over each. Scatter parmesan over, give a grind of black pepper and serve at once.

These can be frozen, uncooked, in individual layers on a tray so they don't all stick together. Once frozen, snap them off and store in the freezer in plastic bags.

THE
LIST

1 kg (2 lb 4 oz) ASPARAGUS

2 TABLESPOONS OLIVE OIL

50 g (1¾ oz) CHOPPED
SPRING ONION (SCALLION)
WITH SOME GREEN PART

2 TABLESPOONS WATER

2 TABLESPOONS
CHOPPED PARSLEY

6 SHEETS (15 x 21 cm/
6 x 8¼ inches) FRESH LASAGNA,
ABOUT 250 g (9 oz)

ABOUT 6 TABLESPOONS
GRATED PARMESAN

4 THIN SLICES
(10 x 18 cm/4 x 7 inches) HAM,
ABOUT 120 g (4¼ oz)

BECHAMEL

60 g (2¼ oz) BUTTER

30 g (1 oz) PLAIN
(ALL-PURPOSE) FLOUR

1 litre (35 fl oz/4 cups) MILK

NUTMEG, FOR GRATING

Serves 6

BARBARA'S ASPARAGUS &
HAM LASAGNA

*My neighbour Barbara makes this whenever asparagus
is in season and we always love it when she brings us a
piece. Use a dish measuring 22 x 30 cm (8½ x 12 inches)
as this will fit everything in. Barbara uses ready-to-bake
lasagna sheets that don't need parboiling first. So easy.*

Snap off the bottom third or so of the asparagus spears.
You won't need these woody parts. Soak the top parts
in a bowl of cold water for 10 minutes or so. Drain in a
colander, then chop them up roughly. Heat the olive oil
in a frying pan and sauté the spring onion until golden.
Add the asparagus and water and cook until softened,
then add the parsley. Season with salt and pepper.
Put the lid on and cook for 10 minutes or so, until the
asparagus are tender but not overcooked.

Preheat the oven to 180°C (350°C/Gas 4). To make the
béchamel, melt the butter in a saucepan and then stir in the
flour. Heat the milk in a separate pot and then slowly pour
into the butter and flour, whisking to loosen it. When the milk
is added and the mixture is smooth, simmer over low heat
for 5 minutes or so to thicken slightly. Season with salt and
pepper, and a grating of nutmeg. Remove from the heat
and stir in the asparagus.

Start the assembly. Spoon a quarter of the béchamel
over the bottom of the dish, spreading it to cover evenly.
Cover with a layer (2 sheets) of pasta, then one-third of
the remaining béchamel, spreading it gently. Scatter
2 tablespoons of parmesan over evenly. Tear 2 slices of
ham in half and make a layer on top of the parmesan.
Add another layer of pasta, half the remaining béchamel,
2 tablespoons of parmesan, then 2 slices of ham. Make
a final layer of pasta, spread with the last of the béchamel
and scatter over the remaining parmesan.

Bake in the oven for 20 minutes or so, until a bit crusty
and golden here and there. Cool a little before cutting
into squares to serve.

PASTA AL FORNO SICILIANA

3 TABLESPOONS OLIVE OIL

1 ONION, CHOPPED

2 GARLIC CLOVES, CHOPPED

1.2 kg (2 lb 10 oz) MINCED (GROUND) BEEF

½ TEASPOON CHOPPED OREGANO

½ TEASPOON CHOPPED THYME

1 BAY LEAF

250 ml (9 fl oz/1 cup) RED WINE

500 ml (17 fl oz/2 cups) TOMATO PASSATA (PUREED TOMATOES)

250 ml (9 fl oz/1 cup) WATER

200 g (7 oz) FROZEN PEAS

450 g (1 lb) RIGATONI PASTA

150 g (5½ oz) THINLY SLICED HAM, TORN UP

250 g (9 oz) MOZZARELLA, ROUGHLY CHOPPED

ABOUT 4 TABLESPOONS GRATED PARMESAN, PLUS EXTRA, FOR SERVING

Serves a neighbourhood

This is what my Sicilian friends have for Sunday lunch. Traditionally, there are larger chunks of meat in the ragù, along with sausage and sometimes slices of boiled egg. It's normally followed by a crumbed meat or chicken cutlet and green salad. They say the lettuce is always there, one way or another. You'll need a 6 cm (2½ inch) high, 30 x 22 cm (12 x 8½ inch) baking dish.

Heat the oil in a deep frying pan and sauté the onion until golden. Add the garlic and sauté until it smells good, then add the minced beef. Brown the beef over quite a high heat, stirring often to break up any lumps. Stir in the oregano, thyme and bay leaf, and season with salt and pepper. Stir through the wine and when that has been absorbed, add the passata and water. Cover and simmer for an hour, stirring now and then. It must be a lovely loose ragù, so add a little water towards the end of cooking if necessary. Toss the peas in and remove from the heat.

Preheat the oven to 190°C (375°F/Gas 5).

Bring a large pot of salted water to the boil and cook the rigatoni to a couple of minutes short of the instructions on the packet. Drain.

Scoop a couple of ladlefuls of the ragù onto the bottom of the dish. Add half the pasta, pressing it along to level it. Ladle over half the remaining ragù and top with all the ham. Scatter half the mozzarella over, then follow with 2 tablespoons of parmesan. Now add the rest of the pasta and press it down firmly. Scrape out the rest of the ragù over the top. Scatter the remaining mozzarella and parmesan over. Bake for 20–30 minutes, until it is a bit crusty on top here and there, and golden around the edges. Scoop out portions and serve with extra parmesan.

PENNE WITH CALAMARI, ZUCCHINI & THEIR FLOWERS

600 g (1 lb 5 oz/ABOUT 8) SMALL CALAMARI (SQUID)

ABOUT 8 LOVELY LARGE ZUCCHINI (COURGETTE) FLOWERS

5 TABLESPOONS OLIVE OIL, PLUS EXTRA, FOR SERVING

6 SMALL ZUCCHINI (COURGETTES) (ABOUT 400 g/ 14 oz), SLICED INTO ROUNDS

3 GARLIC CLOVES, CHOPPED

PINCH OF GROUND CHILLI

3 TABLESPOONS CHOPPED PARSLEY

3 TABLESPOONS WHITE WINE

320 g (11¼ oz) PENNE RIGATE

GRATED PARMESAN, TO SERVE, IF YOU LIKE

Serves 4

Nice, summery and so simple, especially if you have zucchini growing in abundance. It's also a good way of using some of those flowers that dress up the garden. Parmesan may not usually be served with this on account of the calamari, but I think it adds a lovely extra layer. You decide.

Clean the calamari. Remove the ink sac and the beaky part around the tentacles. Keep small tentacles whole and halve them if big. Pull out and discard the transparent quill and rinse the calamari well. Slice the body into rings and keep on a plate with the tentacles.

Rinse the zucchini flowers and remove the inner parts. Cut each flower into 3–4 chunks. Keep aside on paper towels. Meanwhile, heat 3 tablespoons of olive oil in a large frying pan and add the zucchini rounds and half the garlic. Season with some salt and sauté until the zucchini are cooked and golden in parts. Add the flowers and cook for just a moment. Scrape out into a bowl. Add the last 2 tablespoons of oil and the remaining garlic to the pan. When the garlic smells good, add the calamari and sauté for a minute or two. Season with the chilli and salt and pepper. Add 1 tablespoon of the parsley and the wine and cook for a couple of minutes, until the wine reduces.

Meanwhile, bring a pot of salted water to the boil and cook the penne to *al dente*. Return the zucchini to the pan with the calamari and heat for a couple of minutes. Scoop out the pasta with a slotted spoon and mix with the calamari and zucchini, adding a little of the pasta cooking water to help it move smoothly along its way. Add the rest of the parsley, tossing it through gently and evenly. Serve in warm wide pasta bowls, with a drizzle of olive oil, a good grind of pepper and a little grated parmesan, if you wish.

SPAGHETTI
WITH LENTIL RAGU

200 g (7 oz) SMALL
BROWN LENTILS

CLUMP OF FRESH SAGE

1 WHOLE GARLIC CLOVE, PEELED

3 TABLESPOONS OLIVE OIL

1 RED ONION, CHOPPED

400 g (14 oz) TIN
CHOPPED TOMATOES

GOOD PINCH OF GROUND CHILLI

2 TABLESPOONS
CHOPPED PARSLEY

400 g (14 oz) SPAGHETTI

FRESHLY GRATED PARMESAN,
TO SERVE, IF YOU LIKE

───────

Serves 5

My friend Anjalika taught me this and it is wonderful. The kind of thing I want to make very often, served with a mixed green salad (see page 102). If you are making and serving the lentils right away, these liquid amounts are good. However, if you will be making the lentils ahead of time they will absorb water as they sit, so you will need to add a little more water when heating through before serving. Sometimes I like to tear in a little fresh mint with the parsley.

Rinse the lentils, pick out and discard any hard odd bits, then put in a pot and cover with water. Add the sage and garlic and simmer, partly covered, for 25 minutes or so. Add a little hot water if the level becomes low and season with salt towards the end of the cooking time. Drain, keeping the cooking water.

Meanwhile, heat the olive oil in a saucepan and sauté the onion, stirring with a wooden spoon, until it is sticky. Add the tomatoes, a dash of salt, pepper and the chilli. Simmer, mashing down any large lumps, for 10 minutes or so, until the tomato has collapsed. Add the lentils, along with about 250 ml (9 fl oz/1 cup) of the cooking water and simmer, uncovered, for another 10 minutes, for all the flavours to combine. Add a drop more water if it looks too tight or cook a little longer if too loose. Stir in the parsley and remove from the heat.

Meanwhile, cook the pasta in boiling salted water to *al dente*. Drain the pasta and serve in warm wide pasta bowls. Ladle some lentil ragù over each (you may have some ragù left over – I like to serve it with boiled potatoes the next day). Some like this spaghetti with parmesan, but others insist it should be served without.

4 TABLESPOONS
OLIVE OIL

1 RED ONION,
FINELY CHOPPED

1 CELERY STICK,
FINELY CHOPPED

1 CARROT, PEELED AND
FINELY CHOPPED

1 GARLIC CLOVE,
CHOPPED

500 g (1 lb 2 oz)
MINCED (GROUND) BEEF

1 ITALIAN PORK SAUSAGE,
ABOUT 100 g (3½ oz),
SKINNED AND CRUMBLED

NUTMEG, FOR GRATING

185 ml (6 fl oz/¾ cup)
RED WINE

300 g (10½ oz) TINNED
CHOPPED TOMATOES

500 ml (17 fl oz/2 cups) MILK

1 QUANTITY GREEN
TAGLIATELLE (PAGE 140)

FRESHLY GRATED PARMESAN,
TO SERVE

Serves 6 abundantly

RAGU WITH MILK &
GREEN TAGLIATELLE

This makes a good and richer-than-usual ragù, on account of using milk instead of water. I love it. For some reason it is wonderful with green (spinach) tagliatelle. You can make this the day before if you want to break up the load — keep in the fridge and just heat through to serve the next day with your pasta.

Heat the oil in a non-stick deep frying pan and sauté the chopped vegetables until they are a bit golden. Add the garlic and sauté until it smells good, then add the minced beef and sausage and sauté until golden and sticky looking. Add salt and pepper, and an exceptionally good grating of nutmeg and turn through well. Add the wine. Let it reduce to almost nothing and then add the tomatoes, letting the flavours meld for a few minutes. Add the milk and bring back to a simmer. Cover with the lid, lower the heat and simmer for about 1¼ hours, until it is lovely and thick and saucy. If it is too dry in the end, add a little milk and keep going.

Warm a large serving bowl. Bring a large pot of salted water to the boil. Add the pasta, dropping it in gently and distributing it evenly so it doesn't clump in a ball. From when it returns to the boil it should take 4 minutes or so to become tender, but taste to check. Scoop out the pasta with a spaghetti fork and toss gently with the hot sauce in the warmed serving bowl. Add a little of the pasta cooking water to help it along its way. Serve at once in warm wide pasta bowls, scattered with grated parmesan.

GREEN TAGLIATELLE

240 g (8½ oz) YOUNG ENGLISH
SPINACH, TRIMMED
(180 g/6¼ oz TRIMMED WEIGHT)

2 EGGS

400 g (14 oz/2⅔ cups) PLAIN
(ALL-PURPOSE) FLOUR, PLUS
A TAD EXTRA, FOR ROLLING

1 TABLESPOON OLIVE OIL

1 TABLESPOON WATER

––––––

Serves 6

This is easier than you might think — the most challenging part is taking the pasta machine out of the box and attaching it to the table. Once you have got over that block it is tremendously therapeutic. You will feel fabulous and may find yourself planning the next flavour of home-made pasta.

Wash the spinach well and drop in a pot of salted boiling water for a few minutes. Drain very well. When cool, squeeze out all the water you can, until your arms almost ache. Put it in a blender with 1 egg and pulse until puréed.

Pile the flour on your work surface. Make a well in the centre and add the puréed spinach, the remaining egg, a pinch of salt, the olive oil and water. Use your hands to mix until combined, then knead until you have a soft, green dough. If it seems too dry, just pat your hands in water and continue. If too wet, pat your hands in flour. Put the ready dough in a bowl and cover with a cloth. Leave it to rest at room temperature for about half an hour or so.

Set up your pasta machine and have a little pile of flour next to you or on a board. Roll out about a quarter of the dough, keeping the rest covered with a tea towel so it doesn't dry out. Feed the rolled dough through the highest setting on the machine. Fold it up again like a book to neaten it and pass it through this setting again. Lower the setting to halfway on the machine and pass the dough through this setting twice, sprinkling a little flour onto the pasta to avoid sticking. Halve the dough now that it is longer to make it more manageable. Lower the setting to the second-lowest one. Pass each sheet through twice to give 2 sheets of about 46 x 11 cm (18 x 4¼ inches). Lay the sheets, without touching, on a lightly floured surface and leave them to dry for 15 minutes or so. Roll out the remaining portions of dough the same way.

Roll a sheet of pasta up loosely from one short end to the other. Without pressing, gently cut it into thin strips, about 1 cm (½ inch) wide, then unfurl them with your fingers. Have a couple of large trays lined with tea towels and scattered lightly with flour. Fluff the pasta out onto the trays with some of the flour so the strips won't stick together. Cut the remaining pasta sheets into strips. They can be cooked whenever you're ready.

SPAGHETTI WITH PANCETTA, PECORINO & ROSEMARY CRUMBS

6 TABLESPOONS OLIVE OIL

2 GARLIC CLOVES, PEELED
AND SQUASHED WITH
THE FLAT OF A KNIFE

80 g (2¾ oz) BREADCRUMBS,
MADE FROM
DAY-OLD CRUSTLESS
COUNTRY-STYLE BREAD

1 TABLESPOON CHOPPED
ROSEMARY

40 g (1½ oz) PANCETTA,
SLICED ABOUT 2 mm (¹⁄₁₆ inch)
THICK, ROUGHLY CUT UP

3 TOMATOES FROM A TIN

A LITTLE GROUND CHILLI

350 g (12 oz) THICK
SPAGHETTI OR PICI

40 g (1½ oz) THINLY SHAVED
MATURE PECORINO
OR PARMESAN

Serves 4

This is my sister-in-law Luisa's recipe. The tomato here is not much — enough to give just a light coating. Use a day-old country-style bread for the crumbs. The kind of pasta that Luisa would serve with this is pici, a thick, hand-rolled flour and water pasta that is much appreciated. A thick spaghetti would also be great.

To make the crumbs, drizzle 1 tablespoon of olive oil here and there over the bottom of a large frying pan that will eventually hold all your pasta. Add 1 garlic clove and the breadcrumbs and gently sauté until golden, turning through with a wooden spoon so they all get a turn to tan evenly. Add the rosemary and a little salt (bread in Tuscany is generally unsalted, but if your bread is salted you may not need to add any). When the rosemary smells good and you have turned it through and brought out its flavour, scrape the crumbs into a bowl. Wipe out the frying pan with a paper towel and return it to the heat.

Put a pot of salted water on to boil for the pasta. In the frying pan, heat the remaining 5 tablespoons of olive oil with the remaining garlic clove and add the pancetta. Sauté until lightly golden, then add the tomatoes. Break them up with a wooden spoon and simmer for 5 minutes or so, just to warm them in the oil. Season with salt and ground chilli.

Cook the pasta until *al dente*, scoop it out with a spaghetti fork and add to the sauce in the frying pan. Add some of the pasta cooking water to help it along. Turn through to distribute everything evenly, then divide among 4 warm wide pasta bowls. Serve a little per bowl at first, as much of the good sauce goes to the bottom and it's not fair if the last portion gets it all. (In fact, it is said that the guest should get the last plate.) Pile the breadcrumbs over the pasta, heap some shaved pecorino over and give a good grind of black pepper. Serve at once.

SAPIENTE

WORDS/PAROLE

TUTTI I NODI VENGONO AL PETTINE
(All the knots eventually come to the comb)

SPAGHETTI AGLIO, OLIO, PEPERONCINO & AVOCADO

THE
LIST

3 TABLESPOONS OLIVE OIL

1 LARGE GARLIC
CLOVE, CHOPPED

1 SMALL SEMI-DRIED
RED CHILLI, CHOPPED

1 RIPE AVOCADO, NOT TOO BIG

JUICE OF ½ SMALL LEMON

160 g (5½ oz) SPAGHETTI

GRATED PARMESAN, TO SERVE

Serves 2

People are often surprised when I serve this twist on a traditional pasta. It is simple, yet rich and delicious. The avocado has to be a beauty, otherwise forget it. You should be generous with the salt and pepper to bring out its flavour.

Heat the oil and garlic over a very gentle heat in a small frying pan to just draw out the flavour. Take care not to burn the garlic because you can ruin its flavour. When it smells good add the chilli and heat for a moment more. Remove from the heat. Halve the avocado and scoop out nice chunks into a wide serving bowl. Add the lemon juice and season well with salt and pepper.

Meanwhile, cook the pasta in boiling salted water until *al dente*. Pour the cooled garlic and chilli oil over the avocado and gently mix through. Scoop out the pasta with a spaghetti fork directly into the bowl. Add a little of the cooking water to loosen things up and turn through gently, trying to keep the avocado in chunks. Serve immediately with lots of grated parmesan and a nice extra grind of black pepper.

GIOVANNA'S SPAGHETTI

4 TABLESPOONS OLIVE OIL,
PLUS A LITTLE EXTRA, TO SERVE

120 g (4¼ oz) RED
ONION, CHOPPED

100 g (3½ oz) RED PEPPER
(CAPSICUM), CUT INTO
1 cm (½ inch) CHUNKS

180 g (6¼ oz) EGGPLANT
(AUBERGINE), CUT INTO
1 cm (½ inch) CHUNKS

4 ANCHOVY FILLETS, CHOPPED

2 GARLIC CLOVES, CHOPPED

400 g (14 oz) TIN
CHOPPED TOMATOES

2 TABLESPOONS
CHOPPED PARSLEY

1 HEAPED TABLESPOON
EACH OF PITTED GREEN AND
BLACK OLIVES, CHOPPED
BIG OR JUST HALVED

PINCH OF GROUND CHILLI

1 TABLESPOON SMALL CAPERS
IN VINEGAR, DRAINED

400 g (14 oz) SPAGHETTI

1 TABLESPOON
MARJORAM LEAVES

FRESHLY GRATED
PARMESAN, TO SERVE

Serves 5

Giovanna is an incredible, tireless nonna who just gives and gives. This is abundant, packed with goodies and full of flavour. The sauce goes well anytime but particularly in summer when peppers and eggplants are at their best. Use basil instead of the marjoram, if you prefer.

Heat the olive oil in a frying pan that's large enough to hold your spaghetti later. Sauté the onion until softened and light golden. Add the pepper and eggplant and sauté until nicely cooked and a bit sticky. Add the anchovies and garlic, stirring briefly but well to make sure they simmer in the oil. When they smell good add the tomatoes, parsley, olives and a little salt (remember you have the olives and anchovies). Add the chilli and a couple of twists of pepper. Swish out the tomato tin with a little water and pour it in. Cover and simmer for just under 10 minutes, until the sauce is loosely together but not too reduced. Add the capers when it is almost ready, then check the seasoning.

Cook the spaghetti in boiling salted water until *al dente*. Scoop out the pasta with a spaghetti fork directly into the pan of sauce, along with some of the cooking water so it's nice and loose but not too watered down. Tear up the marjoram leaves over and toss well. Divide among warm wide pasta bowls. Serve hot with a small dribble of olive oil, a scattering of parmesan and an extra twist of pepper.

SPAGHETTI WITH CLAMS, TOMATO & A DASH OF CREAM

500 g (1 lb 2 oz) SMALL
CLAMS (VONGOLE VERACI)

2 GARLIC CLOVES,
PEELED, 1 LEFT WHOLE
AND 1 CHOPPED

3 TABLESPOONS OLIVE OIL

200 g (7 oz) CHOPPED TOMATOES

GOOD PINCH OF
GROUND CHILLI

2 TABLESPOONS POURING
(WHIPPING) CREAM

CLUMP OF PARSLEY
WITH STALKS

60 ml (2 fl oz/¼ cup)
WHITE WINE

160 g (5½ oz) THICK SPAGHETTI

2 TABLESPOONS
CHOPPED PARSLEY

Serves 2

Spaghetti with clams in one way or another is always popular. Here, tomatoes and just a little cream bring it together. The clams are cooked separately to the tomatoes in case they dislodge sand.

Soak the clams in a large bowl of cold salted water for a couple of hours to get rid of any sand. Give them a good swishing around in the soaking water a few times and change the water if there is any sand. Discard any clams that are well opened.

In a large frying pan that will hold all the pasta later, stir the chopped garlic in 2 tablespoons of olive oil until it smells good. Add the tomatoes and season with salt and pepper and the chilli. Simmer for just under 10 minutes, squashing any tomato lumps with a wooden spoon. Add the cream and heat through, then remove from the heat.

In another pan that has a lid, heat the last tablespoon of olive oil with the whole garlic clove. When the garlic has perfumed the oil add the drained clams, parsley clump and a grind of pepper. Pour in the wine. Put the lid on and turn the heat right up to steam the clams open. This should only take 5 minutes or so. Check to see if they've opened and give it a couple more minutes for any that haven't. Remove from the heat and cool a tad. Discard any clams that haven't opened. When they are cool enough to handle, pluck out around half of the clam meat, putting it back in the pan and discarding those shells. Leave the rest of the clams in their shells in the pan. Remove the whole garlic clove and parsley clump. Add the clams to the tomato pan, checking as you pour that there is no sand on the bottom of the pan and therefore giving no need to filter in the clam water.

Bring a pot of salted water to the boil and cook the spaghetti to *al dente*. When the pasta is just about ready, put the pan holding the clams over a high flame to heat through, then add the drained spaghetti. Turn through well. Let it heat through for a minute, then scatter with the chopped parsley and serve at once with a good grind of black pepper. Serve with a plate for the shells.

SPAGHETTI WITH
CLAMS & TABASCO

500 g (1 lb 2 oz) SMALL CLAMS
(VONGOLE VERACI)

1 GARLIC CLOVE, CHOPPED

2 TABLESPOONS OLIVE OIL,
PLUS EXTRA, FOR SERVING

CLUMP OF PARSLEY
WITH STALKS

3 TABLESPOONS WHITE WINE

160 g (5½ oz) SPAGHETTI

½ TABLESPOON
CHOPPED PARSLEY

TABASCO SAUCE, TO SERVE

Serves 2

Here is a can't-get-simpler way with clams that has a good kick. Some people may like a squeeze of lemon juice over their serving. Follow on from here with a strongly flavoured dish that won't pale.

Soak the clams in a large bowl of cold salted water for a couple of hours to get rid of any sand. Give them a good swishing around in the soaking water a few times and change the water if there is any sand. Discard any clams that are well opened.

In a large frying pan that will hold all your pasta later, heat the garlic in the olive oil until it smells good. Add the drained clams, parsley clump, wine and a grind of pepper. Cover and turn the heat right up to steam the clams open. This should only take 5 minutes or so. Check to see if they've opened and give it a couple more minutes for any that haven't. Remove from the heat and cool a tad.

Discard any clams that haven't opened. When they are cool enough to handle, pluck out around half of the clam meat, putting it back in the pan and discarding those shells. Leave the rest of the clams in their shells in the pan. Remove the parsley clump. Check that there is no sand on the bottom of the pan and therefore no need to filter in the clam water.

Bring a pot of salted water to the boil and cook the spaghetti to *al dente*. When the pasta is just about ready, put the pan holding the clams over a high flame to heat through, then add the drained spaghetti. Turn through well and let it heat together for a minute. Scatter with just enough parsley to add a dash of colour and serve at once with a grind of black pepper and a good shake of Tabasco — as much as you can take. Serve with an extra drizzle of olive oil and a plate for the shells.

TORTA DI SPAGHETTI

600 g (1 lb 5 oz) LEFTOVER
COOKED PASTA
(250 g/9 oz UNCOOKED)

2 TABLESPOONS OLIVE OIL

4 EGGS

4 TABLESPOONS GRATED
PARMESAN, PLUS A LITTLE
EXTRA, TO SERVE (OPTIONAL)

A FEW HERBS, CHOPPED

Serves 4

This is the thing to make when you have leftover pasta (okay, so you need a lot of it, but you never know). Or when you have an empty pan with some sauce clinging to it — scrape up all the clinging good stuff that was about to get rinsed out in the dishwater, it's such a potential building block. Of course, you can also make this from scratch, as I have often been asked to do by my children. Don't worry too much about precise amounts, it should just cover the bottom of the pan. You can get more elaborate and add mozzarellas and salamis, but that is another thing. Here is the basic route.

Have the cooked pasta at room temperature. Heat the oil in a 26 cm (10½ inch) non-stick pan and swizzle it around.

Add the pasta, flattening it like a neat nest. Whip the eggs in a bowl with a little salt. Pour out evenly over the pasta and turn through to make sure all the pasta is coated. Flatten again. Fry for a couple of minutes, then scatter the parmesan and herbs evenly over the top. Cook for a couple of minutes more, until the egg is set and a bit crusty in places. Put the lid on and leave the pan off the heat for 5 minutes or longer, so the cheese melts a bit.

Loosen the edges with a wooden spatula, slipping it all the way underneath to make sure nothing is stuck. Have a large plate ready. Put the lid on the pan and flip the pan over so the torta is upside down on the lid. Now put the serving plate upside down over the torta and flip it back over with as much finesse as you can manage. Cut slices with a sharp knife and serve with a spatula. Serve hot with an extra scattering of parmesan if you like.

BARBARA'S MUM'S
SPINACH POLPETTINE

650 g (1 lb 7 oz) YOUNG ENGLISH
SPINACH, TRIMMED
(500 g/1 lb 2 oz
TRIMMED WEIGHT)

250 g (9 oz) FRESH RICOTTA

NUTMEG, FOR GRATING

2 TABLESPOONS GRATED
PARMESAN, PLUS EXTRA,
FOR SERVING

1 EGG, LIGHTLY WHIPPED

5 TABLESPOONS OLIVE OIL

1 GARLIC CLOVE, PEELED
AND SQUASHED WITH
THE FLAT OF A KNIFE

400 g (14 oz) TIN
CHOPPED TOMATOES

A FEW BASIL LEAVES, TORN

Serves 3–4

*This recipe comes from Diana, my neighbour's mum.
She is a great cook. It's very easy to make, with only a
few ingredients, and it is healthy and always appreciated.
Serve as a first course instead of pasta or rice.*

Cook the spinach in boiling salted water for a few minutes.
Drain it very well, pressing out the water. Cool, then chop it
up fine and put in a bowl. Add the ricotta, a good grating
of nutmeg, the parmesan and egg, mixing it all well
together. Taste for salt and pepper.

Preheat the oven to 180°C (350°F/Gas 4).

Heat 3 tablespoons of olive oil in a saucepan with the
squashed garlic. Add the tomatoes and basil and season
with salt and a little pepper. Swirl about 125 ml (4 fl oz/
½ cup) of water around in the tomato tin and add that
too. Simmer for 5 minutes or so. If there are still big bits of
tomato, crush them with a fork or potato masher. Remove
from the heat.

Drizzle the remaining 2 tablespoons of olive oil into an
oval baking dish, roughly 26 x 14 cm (10½ x 5½ inches).
Spoon about one-third of the tomato sauce over the
bottom of the dish. Take a tablespoon of the spinach mix
and edge it off gently with another spoon onto the tomato
sauce in the dish. Continue with the remaining spinach
mix, resting the balls in compact rows. You will have about
16 balls. Dollop the rest of the tomato sauce over the balls.
It's best if most of them are covered, at least in part.
Bake for 20–25 minutes, until a bit golden here and there.
Serve warm, scattered with parmesan.

RISOTTO WITH PRAWNS, LAVENDER & LEMON

700 g (1 lb 9 oz) MEDIUM
RAW PRAWNS (SHRIMP)

1.25 litres (44 fl oz/5 cups)
QUICK VEGETABLE
BROTH (PAGE 156)

90 g (3¼ oz) BUTTER

80 g (2¾ oz) SPRING
ONIONS (SCALLIONS)
WITH SOME GREEN,
CHOPPED

320 g (11¼ oz)
RISOTTO RICE (ARBORIO
OR CARNAROLI)

60 ml (2 fl oz/¼ cup)
WHITE WINE

ABOUT 12 FRESH UNSPRAYED
LAVENDER SPRIGS

2 TEASPOONS FINELY
GRATED LEMON RIND,
YELLOW PART ONLY

4 TABLESPOONS
BRANDY

4 TABLESPOONS
POURING (WHIPPING) CREAM

GRATED PARMESAN,
TO SERVE, IF YOU LIKE

Serves 4

This is delicate, summery and delicious. You may like to add a shower of fresh herbs at the end. Have the butter and cream at room temperature.

Shell and devein the prawns, discarding the heads and reserving the shells. Make the vegetable broth, adding the prawn shells to the pot with the vegetables. Keep hot.

Heat 50 g (1¾ oz) of the butter in a large wide pot and sauté the spring onions gently until cooked and pale golden, but not too dark. Add the rice and cook until it starts to stick, turning it through with a wooden spoon. Pour in the wine and cook until it has mostly vanished. Add 500 ml (17 fl oz/2 cups) of the hot broth and simmer, stirring now and then with a wooden spoon, until the liquid has been absorbed by the rice. Add another 250 ml (9 fl oz/1 cup) of broth and 2–4 of the lavender sprigs. Depending on your broth you may need to add salt and pepper here. Once this broth has been gently absorbed, continue to add more broth, letting it simmer and absorb before adding the next cupful. The risotto is ready when the rice is creamy, yet still a little firm, and there is just a small amount of liquid in the pot, about 20 minutes. If you run out of broth, you can use hot water.

Meanwhile, put a non-stick frying pan over high heat with half the remaining butter and when it's hot, add the prawns. Sauté until they are opaque and a bit golden on both sides. Add 1 teaspoon of the lemon rind with a little salt and pepper and toss together. Add the brandy and stand well back as if it flames up it can be very exaggerated. Let it evaporate, then turn off the heat.

Add the cream and the last of the butter to the risotto. Turn through to finish, or *mantecare* as they say in Italy. Scrape in the prawns and the other teaspoon of lemon rind and heat through just for a couple of minutes to amalgamate all the flavours. Taste and adjust the seasoning. Add extra hot water or broth if the risotto is too stiff. Remove the lavender and serve at once, with some fresh lavender sprigs on top. Give a good grinding of black pepper and scatter with parmesan, if you wish.

RISOTTO WITH PEARS & PECORINO

4 TABLESPOONS OLIVE OIL

1 BULB SPRING ONION
(SCALLION), CHOPPED

320 g (11¼ oz) RISOTTO RICE
(ARBORIO OR CARNAROLI)

125 ml (4 fl oz/½ cup)
WHITE WINE

2 (ABOUT 350 g/12 oz IN TOTAL)
LOVELY RIPE PEARS

1.25 litres (44 fl oz/5 cups)
QUICK VEGETABLE BROTH
(SEE BELOW), HOT

80 g (2¾ oz) FRESH PECORINO,
CHOPPED INTO CUBES

40 g (1½ oz) GRATED
MATURE PECORINO

80 g (2¾ oz) OR SO SHAVED
MATURE PECORINO

GROUND CINNAMON, TO SERVE

Serves 4

I use two types of pecorino here – a fresher one to turn through the risotto and melt a bit, and a good firmer mature one for grating in and shaving on top. You can use parmesan if you can't find a mature pecorino. I love this with a dusting of cinnamon, as I ate it in a restaurant – try it with and without to see which way you prefer.

Heat the olive oil in a large wide pot and sauté the spring onion until pale golden and softened. Add the rice and cook for a couple of minutes, stirring. Next, add the wine and let it sizzle and evaporate. Peel, core and chop 1 of the pears into cubes, then add to the pan. Turn through to blend the flavours, then add about 500 ml (17 fl oz/ 2 cups) of the broth. When that has been absorbed, add another cup or so of broth. Depending on your broth you may need to add salt and pepper here. When this broth has been gently absorbed continue to add more, letting it simmer and absorb before adding the next cupful. The risotto is ready when the rice is creamy, yet still a little firm, and there is just a small amount of liquid in the pot, about 20 minutes. If you run out of broth, you can use hot water.

Peel, core and chop up the second pear and add it to the risotto along with the fresh pecorino. Turn through to meld the flavours, then stir in the grated mature pecorino. Serve up immediately, dividing the shaved pecorino over the top, then adding a dusting of cinnamon for whoever wants it and a generous grind of black pepper over each.

QUICK VEGETABLE BROTH

1.75 litres (61 fl oz/
7 cups) WATER

1 CARROT

1 SMALL ONION, PEELED

1 CELERY STICK

1 WHOLE GARLIC CLOVE, PEELED

A FEW PEPPERCORNS

HANDFUL OF FRESH HERBS

Makes about 1.25 litres

Put all the ingredients, except the herbs, in a pot with some salt and bring to the boil. Skim the surface if necessary, then simmer for about 30 minutes. Add the herbs to infuse for the last 5 minutes or so. Strain to use.

— THE —

Dining Room

— POULTRY & RABBIT —

CHICKEN WITH PEPPERS

RABBIT, PANCETTA & ROSEMARY PATE

MARISA'S ROAST CHICKEN

BAKED CRUMBED CHICKEN WITH MOZZARELLA,
ANCHOVIES & CAPERS

CHICKEN BREAST PIE WITH PORCINI & SAGE

CHICKEN WITH SALSICCIA & FENNEL

GRILLED GALLETTI

CHICKEN CIABATTA WITH VALERIANA,
PECORINO & HAZELNUT SALAD

COLLO RIPIENO

ROAST LEMON & THYME CHICKEN

ROAST RABBIT WITH GRAPES

STUFFED GUINEA FOWL

SAPIENTE

WORDS/PAROLE

DRINK A MIXTURE OF
1 TEASPOON VINEGAR AND
1 TEASPOON SUGAR TO
STOP HICCUPS

CHICKEN
WITH PEPPERS

3 LARGE PEPPERS (CAPSICUMS),
2 RED AND 1 YELLOW

1 x 1.3 kg (3 lb) CHICKEN,
SKIN REMOVED, CUT
INTO 8 OR SO PIECES

10 WHOLE GARLIC CLOVES,
UNPEELED

3 FRESH BAY LEAVES

3 ROSEMARY BRANCHES

100 g (3½ oz) GOOD
BLACK OLIVES

4 TABLESPOONS
OLIVE OIL

Makes 4 big serves

If you love peppers, you will love this. It looks like it almost cooked itself and came right to your table. It is perfect in summer when peppers are ripe and at their best. You can just pile all the ingredients in, put it in the oven and then lie down and read a book. There is nothing else to do.

Preheat the oven to 180°C (350°F/Gas 4). Halve the peppers, remove the seeds and chop each half into about 4 rustic pieces. Put in a 30 x 23 cm (12 x 9 inch) casserole dish and add the chicken, garlic, bay leaves, rosemary, olives and olive oil. Season with salt and pepper and turn it all through with your hands. If it really is too tight to turn, mix in a large bowl and return to the dish. Cover with the lid. Put in the oven and bake for about 1½ hours or until the chicken is cooked through and soft and the peppers are gorgeous.

Take the lid off and bake for another 20 minutes or so to give some blush to the chicken. Serve warm, with bread. Bread here is essential. If the skin of the peppers is starting to come away and it bothers you, just slip it to the side of the plate.

RABBIT, PANCETTA & ROSEMARY PATE

THE LIST

1 RABBIT, CUT UP INTO
8–10 PIECES

ABOUT 1 litre
(35 fl oz/4 cups) WATER

400 g (14 oz) SLICED
ROUND PANCETTA

1 ONION, PEELED

2 WHOLE GARLIC
CLOVES, PEELED

1 HEAPED TABLESPOON
CHOPPED ROSEMARY

1½ TEASPOONS FINE SALT

5–6 BLACK PEPPERCORNS

Serves many

This recipe comes from Lydia's friend. She always makes a double dose and takes one to a friend. You could use a pressure cooker to shorten the cooking time. If so, add just enough liquid to cover. Serve this with grilled bread.

Rinse the rabbit under cold water and remove any fat and unwanted bits. Put in a pot with the water. Roll up the pancetta slices a few at a time and cut with kitchen scissors into the pot. Add the onion, garlic, rosemary, salt and peppercorns. Bring to the boil. Cover and simmer until the rabbit is very tender, about 1 hour 15 minutes. Remove the rabbit pieces (keeping the liquid) and cool a little, but they should still be a bit warm when you clean and purée them.

Remove the meat from the rabbit bones. Squelch the meat through your fingers (this is rather therapeutic) into a bowl to make sure no small bits of bone remain. Be thorough. Put the pancetta, onion and cleaned rabbit meat in the bowl of a food processor and add about 185 ml (6 fl oz/¾ cup) of the cooking water. Pulse to blend the mixture to a smooth purée. Taste for seasoning.

Line a 30 x 11 x 6 cm (12 x 4¼ x 2½ inch) loaf tin with a double thickness of baking paper. Leave some overhang on the long sides. Scrape the rabbit purée in and smooth the surface. Fold the overhanging baking paper across to cover the top, then put the tin in the fridge overnight.

To serve, lift the pâté from the tin using the overhanging paper and turn upside down onto a plate. Top with a few good grinds of pepper. Serve at room temperature with grilled bread and a nice salad.

SAPIENTE
WORDS/PAROLE

**MEGLIO UN UOVO OGGI
CHE UNA GALLINA DOMANI**

*(Better an egg today than
a hen tomorrow)*

MARISA'S
ROAST
CHICKEN

1 CHICKEN, ABOUT
1.4 kg (3 lb 2 oz)

2 TABLESPOONS OLIVE OIL

1½ TABLESPOONS ROSEMARY
& SAGE SALT (PAGE 24)

Serves 4

*This is plain, rustic, simple and healthy on account
of having hardly any oil. It is nice with olive mash
(see page 239) or a potato salad.*

Preheat the oven to 200°C (400°F/Gas 6). Rinse the
chicken and pat dry with paper towels. Flick a little water
onto the bottom of a roasting dish and cover with a piece
of baking paper. Drizzle the oil over the chicken, add the
herbed salt and rub all over the skin. Put in the roasting
dish, breast up, and roast for about 30 minutes. Baste,
then pour off the excess liquid from the bottom of the
dish and return the chicken to the oven, basting a couple
of times more, for a further 40 minutes or until it is cooked
through, crusty and golden. Cut the chicken into pieces
so it's quick and easy to serve.

BAKED CRUMBED CHICKEN WITH MOZZARELLA, ANCHOVIES & CAPERS

4 SINGLE SKINLESS CHICKEN
BREAST FILLETS, TRIMMED OF
ANY FAT AND BITS OF BONE

3 TABLESPOONS
CHOPPED PARSLEY

1 TEASPOON CHOPPED THYME

1 GARLIC CLOVE, CHOPPED

4 ANCHOVY FILLETS, DRAINED,
CHOPPED BUT NOT TOO FINE

1 TEASPOON CAPERS IN
VINEGAR, DRAINED, CHOPPED

100 g (3½ oz) MOZZARELLA,
CUT INTO SMALL DICE

80 g (2¾ oz/2 LARGE SLICES)
DAY-OLD CRUSTLESS
COUNTRY-STYLE BREAD

1 HEAPED TABLESPOON
GRATED PARMESAN

1 EGG

4 TABLESPOONS OLIVE OIL

20 g (¾ oz) BUTTER

Serves 4

These buttery crumbed chicken breasts, stuffed with mozzarella, anchovies and herbs, go well served with a gentle pile of mashed potatoes. The thin strip on the underside of the chicken breast that cuts away naturally (tenderloin) is not needed here. Use it in a soup or risotto, or to make mini fried chicken schnitzels for small panini.

Preheat the oven to 180°C (350°F/Gas 4). Wipe the chicken breasts clean with paper towels. Cut a long deep pocket in each one through the thickest side, being careful not to cut all the way through or the filling will ooze out. Scatter a little salt and pepper over both sides of the chicken. Mix 1 tablespoon of the parsley with the thyme, garlic, anchovies, capers and mozzarella in a small bowl. Divide among the chicken breasts and stuff well into the pockets. Use 2 toothpicks to seal off each opening.

Pulse the bread in a food processor to give uniform soft crumbs. Remove to a plate and mix in the remaining 2 tablespoons of parsley and the parmesan. Lightly beat the egg in a wide bowl with some salt and black pepper. Dip the chicken breasts in the egg and then pat gently into the crumbs, helping them stick with your hands.

Put 2 tablespoons of the oil and the butter in a baking dish just large enough to hold the chicken snugly. Add the chicken, drizzle over the remaining 2 tablespoons of oil and bake for 30 minutes or longer, until deep golden and slightly crispy. Remove from the oven and rest, covered with foil, for 5 minutes or so. Remove the toothpicks and slice each breast on the diagonal into about 6 slices. Put on serving plates, drizzle each with a little juice from the pan and give a final grind of black pepper. Serve with a squeeze of lemon juice if you like.

CHICKEN BREAST PIE
WITH PORCINI & SAGE

◇◇

THE
LIST

2 SINGLE SKINLESS CHICKEN
BREAST FILLETS, TRIMMED OF
ANY FAT AND BITS OF BONE

2 TABLESPOONS OLIVE OIL

4 LARGE THYME SPRIGS

4 LARGE SAGE LEAVES

1 ROSEMARY BRANCH,
NOT TOO LARGE

80 g (2¾ oz) MASCARPONE

250 g (9 oz) POLISH PUFF PASTRY
(PAGE 51)

1 EGG, LIGHTLY BEATEN,
FOR BRUSHING

200 g (7 oz) FRESH
PORCINI MUSHROOMS

3 TABLESPOONS OLIVE OIL

1 GARLIC CLOVE, PEELED
AND SQUASHED WITH
THE FLAT OF A KNIFE

6–8 SAGE LEAVES

Serves 2–3

I love savoury food wrapped in pastry. These chicken breasts are coated in herbs and mascarpone before being wrapped in pastry and baked. If you don't want to make your own puff pastry, just use a bought one. You can use any fresh mushrooms if you can't get fresh porcini.

Salt and pepper the chicken breasts well on all sides. Heat the oil in a non-stick frying pan and when hot add the chicken. Cook until nicely golden on all sides. They will finish cooking in the oven but they must have a good crust. Remove to a plate to cool.

Preheat the oven to 200°C (400°F/Gas 6). Strip the herbs off their stems and chop them up together. You'll need about 2 tablespoons. Mix into the mascarpone with a little salt. Cut the pastry in half and roll each out into a rectangle large enough to wrap a chicken breast.

Spread one-quarter of the mascarpone mix onto the middle of each rectangle in a square that the chicken will sit on. Put the chicken on top and spread with the remaining mascarpone. Carefully wrap up the pastry in a good parcel around the chicken, not too tightly or the chicken might burst out, and making sure that it is generous at the seam. Put the parcels on a baking tray lined with baking paper. Brush the top of each with egg and bake for about 25 minutes or longer if necessary, until the pastry is puffed, golden and glossy. Remove from the oven and rest for 10–15 minutes before serving.

Meanwhile, cut off the porcini stems and slice thickly, along with the caps. Heat the olive oil in a large non-stick frying pan over high heat and add the garlic and porcini stems. Sauté until the garlic smells good, then add the caps. Continue cooking and when the porcini brown a little, add the sage. Cook, stirring, until the sage is crisp.

Serve whole or in slices of 1–2 cm (½–¾ inch), with the hot porcini on the side.

CHICKEN WITH SALSICCIA & FENNEL

1.2 kg (2 lb 10 oz) CHICKEN,
SKIN REMOVED,
CUT UP INTO 8 PIECES

2 FENNEL BULBS (ABOUT
200 g/7 oz EACH)

3 TABLESPOONS OLIVE OIL

1 WHITE ONION, CHOPPED

1 CELERY STICK, CHOPPED

1 LARGE GARLIC
CLOVE, CHOPPED

3 ITALIAN PORK SAUSAGES
(ABOUT 100 g/3½ oz
EACH), SKINNED

125 ml (4 fl oz/½ cup)
WHITE WINE

1 TEASPOON FENNEL
SEEDS, CRUSHED

ABOUT 500 ml (17 fl oz/
2 cups) HOT WATER

Serves 4

This dish is lovely with potatoes, either mashed or boiled, cooked greens and bread for the juice.

Rinse the chicken and pat dry with paper towels. Rinse and trim the fennel, keeping the fronds. Cut the fennel lengthways into quarters, keeping the quarters joined at the bottom. Heat the oil in a large frying pan and sauté the onion and celery until golden. Add the garlic and cook until it smells good, then crumble the sausages into the pan. Cook until they have taken on a good colour. Add the chicken and sauté until golden in parts.

Add the wine and let it evaporate, then add the fennel quarters, crushed fennel seeds and salt and pepper. Pour in the water, cover with the lid and simmer for 45 minutes to an hour. Take the lid off for the last 10 minutes to reduce any thin sauce – the end result must be saucy, but not too liquid. Remove from the heat. Tear in a few fennel fronds here and there. Serve with bread.

SAPIENTE

WORDS/PAROLE

DON'T KINDLE A FIRE THAT
YOU CAN'T PUT OUT

GRILLED GALLETTI

These are tender, marinated poussins that are cooked under the oven grill. Not too chilli or herby, but delicate and just the right flavour. You can cook them on a barbecue if you like.

Cut the galletti down the backbone and open out to flatten. Rinse and pat dry with paper towels. Salt and pepper both sides, then lay them in an oven dish large enough to take them side by side.

Mix the lemon juice, olive oil, chilli, Tabasco sauce and rosemary together in a bowl and pour over the galletti. Tuck the bay leaf and garlic in between. Massage the flavourings into the galletti well, making sure all sides are covered. Leave them skin side up. Cover the dish with plastic wrap and put in the fridge for at least an hour, but as long as overnight.

Preheat the oven grill. Turn the galletti skin side down. When the grill is hot, put the oven dish under and grill the galletti for about 45 minutes, turning them after 25 minutes or when brown on the top. Continue grilling, skin side up now, until the skin is crisp and golden. Towards the end of grilling you may need to add a little water to the dish to prevent the sauce drying out too much. Remove from the grill and rest for 10 minutes before serving. Serve with a salad with fresh blossoms.

THE LIST

2 GALLETTI
(BABY CHICKENS/POUSSINS),
460 g (1 lb ¼ oz) EACH

JUICE OF 1 LEMON

4 TABLESPOONS OLIVE OIL

½ DRIED RED CHILLI WITH
SEEDS, CHOPPED

1 TEASPOON OR SO
TABASCO SAUCE

1 TABLESPOON CHOPPED
ROSEMARY

1 FRESH BAY LEAF,
TORN IN HALF

2 GARLIC CLOVES,
PEELED AND SQUASHED
WITH THE FLAT OF A KNIFE

Serves 2 generously

CHICKEN CIABATTA WITH VALERIANA, PECORINO & HAZELNUT SALAD

THE
LIST

VALERIANA, PECORINO &
HAZELNUT SALAD (PAGE 182)

1 SINGLE SKINLESS CHICKEN
BREAST FILLET

1 EGG

½ TEASPOON CHOPPED THYME

ABOUT ½ teacup
DRY BREADCRUMBS

3 TABLESPOONS
GRATED PARMESAN

OLIVE OIL, FOR FRYING

3 PANINO-SIZED PIECES
OF CIABATTA (PAGE 50)

LEMON WEDGES,
TO SERVE, IF YOU LIKE

Serves 3

I love fried chicken, especially in a ciabatta panino with lots of lemon squeezed in for some moisture and taste, and some salad leaves. This is a little more elaborate. It is lovely when the chicken is warm, but if you need to fry the chicken ahead of time it is also good cold.

Prepare the salad on the plates but don't dress it just yet.

Slice the chicken breast horizontally into 3 portions. They don't have to be exactly the same size, just go with the natural curves where you need to. Pound each one out a little with a meat mallet. Whisk the egg in a bowl with the thyme and a little salt and pepper. Pour into a wide bowl. Put the chicken in the egg and turn to coat all over. (This step can be done in advance — keep in the fridge, covered, until required.)

Mix the breadcrumbs and parmesan together on a flat plate. Lift each piece of chicken from the egg and pat each side firmly into the crumbs. Put the crumbed chicken on a plate. Heat enough oil to cover the bottom of a large frying pan and when it's hot add the chicken. Fry until firm and deep golden on the underside, then turn and cook the other side. Remove to a plate lined with paper towels and keep them warm.

Halve each piece of ciabatta horizontally and fill with the chicken. Now dress the salad and serve it inside the panino or alongside. Squeeze some lemon juice on if you like. Close the panino, squash it so the juices go onto the bread and eat straight away.

VALERIANA, PECORINO & HAZELNUT SALAD

15 g (½ oz) SKINNED HAZELNUTS,
ROUGHLY CHOPPED

75 g (2¾ oz) MATURE PECORINO

40 g (1½ oz) SPRING ONIONS
(SCALLIONS), TRIMMED

50 g (1¾ oz) VALERIANA
(LAMB'S LETTUCE)
OR WATERCRESS

2–3 TABLESPOONS OLIVE OIL

JUICE OF ABOUT ½ LEMON

Serves 3

*This is my friend Lisa's addition to our chicken ciabatta.
She likes to layer her salad in this way. I love the details
of keeping the white and green onion rings separate,
and separating the individual rings. So much gentler
in the mouth.*

Toast the hazelnuts lightly in a dry frying pan, taking care
not to take them too far as this will make them bitter. Keep
aside. Shave the pecorino thinly on the slotted side of a
cheese grater, or with a potato peeler if you prefer. It looks
good when the shavings are not uniform. Thinly slice the
spring onions, keeping the white and green parts separate.

Divide the valeriana among 3 serving plates. Scatter
the white onion rings over, separating them out into
individual rings. Drizzle each salad with about 3 teaspoons
of olive oil and squeeze a little lemon juice over each. Add
generous grindings of salt and black pepper. Top with
shavings of pecorino, then the green part of the spring
onions and finally, garnish with the hazelnuts. Gently toss
the salad on the plate before eating.

SAPIENTE

WORDS/PAROLE

WASTE NOT,
WANT NOT

2 CHICKEN NECKS WITH
HEADS ATTACHED

1 CARROT

1 CELERY STICK

1 ONION

STUFFING

130 g (4½ oz) MINCED
(GROUND) BEEF

40 g (1½ oz) ITALIAN PORK
SAUSAGE, PROSCIUTTO OR
MORTADELLA, CHOPPED

150 g (5½ oz) CHICKEN LIVERS,
TRIMMED AND CHOPPED

75 g (2¾ oz) CRUSTLESS DAY-OLD
BREAD, SOAKED IN MILK FOR
30 MINUTES AND SQUEEZED DRY

40 g (1½ oz) GRATED PARMESAN

2 EGGS

GOOD GRATING OF NUTMEG

GRATED RIND OF 1 LEMON,
YELLOW PART ONLY

Serves 2

COLLO RIPIENO

This is a very authentic Tuscan housewives' recipe, with the mentality of not wasting anything. You might like to try it if you get your chickens whole. It has a rather old-fashioned feeling. Wilma recommends serving it with salsa verde (see page 18) and preserved vegetables (see page 14). Cut the chicken necks off so they're as long as possible.

Wash the chicken necks, then slide the inner bones out of each one. Tie off the heads at the end of the necks to ensure the stuffing stays in the necks. Mix everything for the stuffing together well. Stuff the necks, but don't exaggerate the amount or they could tear during cooking. Sew the open ends closed so nothing will leak out.

Put a pot of salted water on to boil with the carrot, celery and onion. Add the chicken necks and simmer for about an hour, checking that they stay covered with water throughout. Use a pin to prick the necks to see if they are ready — they are done when no liquid seeps out. Remove from the liquid and cool, so they are easier to slice.

ROAST LEMON
& THYME CHICKEN

1½ LEMONS

1 WHOLE CHICKEN

2 GARLIC CLOVES,
ROUGHLY CHOPPED

3 TABLESPOONS OLIVE OIL

2 SMALL FRESH BAY LEAVES

HANDFUL OF THYME SPRIGS

185 ml (6 fl oz/¾ cup) WATER

2 TABLESPOONS POURING
(WHIPPING) CREAM

SALAD

2 LARGE HANDFULS OF
VALERIANA (LAMB'S LETTUCE)
OR WATERCRESS

2 TABLESPOONS OLIVE OIL

1 TEASPOON DIJON MUSTARD

1 SCANT TABLESPOON
RED WINE VINEGAR

1 GARLIC CLOVE, PEELED
AND SQUASHED WITH
THE FLAT OF A KNIFE

Serves 4

Use a non-stick baking dish, one that will fit the chicken pieces snugly without the pan juices spreading thinly and burning. The dish I use is 22 x 30 cm (8½ x 12 inches).

Cut 8 slices, about 5 mm (¼ inch) thick from the whole lemon. Cut the chicken up into 4 pieces, following the natural curves of bone. Cut away the wing tips. Rinse the pieces and pat dry. Squeeze the lemon half and anything left from the whole lemon into your baking dish and add the chicken pieces, garlic, olive oil, bay leaves and thyme. Add salt and pepper and turn the chicken pieces to coat them well. Leave, skin side up, for 1 hour or so to marinate.

Preheat the oven to 200°C (400°F/Gas 6). Tuck the lemon slices under the chicken with the garlic and thyme. It's good if they see some open air so they get caramelly golden, but not too much or they will burn and become bitter. If you see them burning during roasting, tuck them completely under the chicken. Roast for 30 minutes, then pour 125 ml (4 fl oz/½ cup) of the water around the edges. Roast for another 20–30 minutes, until the skin on top is lovely and crisp and the juices are deep golden and lovely. Add an extra dribble of water in this time if needed.

While the chicken is roasting prepare the salad. Rinse and dry the valeriana and put in a wide bowl ready for tossing later. Whip the oil, mustard and vinegar in a small bowl, then add the garlic and season with salt and pepper. Leave to sit and mingle.

Take the dish from the oven. Remove the chicken and lemon slices to an oval platter and cut the chicken with poultry scissors into smaller pieces. Add the cream and remaining 60 ml (2 fl oz/¼ cup) of water to the dish and put on the stovetop to bubble up and reduce, scraping up any interesting bits caught on the base with a wooden spoon. When you are satisfied with the thickness turn off the heat. Turn the salad through gently with about 2 tablespoons of the dressing — it should be just a light coat, not a dressing gown. Taste and adjust the seasoning if necessary. Divide among serving plates. Add the chicken and drizzle the sauce over. Serve with bread.

SAPIENTE
WORDS/PAROLE

BETTER TO KEEP THE OLD
BROOM THAT SWEEPS WELL
THAN TO GET A NEW ONE

ROAST RABBIT
WITH GRAPES

◇◇

1 RABBIT

5 TABLESPOONS OLIVE OIL

250 ml (9 fl oz/1 cup)
WHITE WINE

ABOUT 20 JUNIPER
BERRIES, SQUASHED WITH
THE FLAT OF A KNIFE

2 GARLIC CLOVES, PEELED
AND SQUASHED WITH
THE FLAT OF A KNIFE

2 BAY LEAVES, TORN

4 THYME SPRIGS, PLUS EXTRA,
TO SERVE, IF YOU LIKE

100 g (3½ oz) PANCETTA,
CHOPPED

500 ml (17 fl oz/2 cups)
WATER

500 g (1 lb 2 oz) BLACK
AND WHITE GRAPES

Serves 4–6

*This is lovely to make in autumn when grapes are
everywhere. I like to use black and white grapes – you
might like to use seedless grapes if you can get them.*

Cut the rabbit up into about 12 pieces and put in a
good-sized bowl with 2 tablespoons of olive oil, the wine,
juniper berries, garlic, bay leaves and thyme, and a few
good grinds of black pepper. Leave, covered, for an hour
or two to marinate, in the fridge if it is a warm day.

Heat the remaining 3 tablespoons of oil in a large deep
pan. Lift the rabbit pieces from the marinade (reserve the
marinade), shake out, then brown well on all sides. Add
the pancetta and fry that too, until golden. Salt the rabbit
pieces, then add the marinade to the pan along with the
water. Cover and simmer for 30 minutes. Add half the
grapes, cover again and simmer for 30–40 minutes or so.
Add the rest of the grapes and simmer, uncovered, for
10 minutes more to slightly thicken the juices in the pan.
Check the seasoning and serve.

STUFFED
GUINEA FOWL

1 GUINEA FOWL

400 g (14 oz) MINCED
(GROUND) BEEF

400 g (14 oz) ITALIAN PORK
SAUSAGE, SKINNED

50 g (1¾ oz) GRATED PARMESAN

3 EGGS, LIGHTLY BEATEN

200 g (7 oz) CRUSTLESS
YESTERDAY'S BREAD, BATHED
IN MILK TO COVER

1 TABLESPOON TRUFFLE
BUTTER (PAGE 19), SOFTENED

PINCH OF NUTMEG

4 TABLESPOONS OLIVE OIL

250 ml (9 fl oz/1 cup)
WHITE WINE

Serves 6–8

This is my sister-in-law Luisa's wonderful recipe. She makes it for Christmas. Something like this is always elegant. I love to serve it with a variety of vegetables, especially cardoons.

Have your butcher debone the guinea fowl, keeping the skin intact. Keep the bones. You can do this yourself if you know how. Flame the skin side if it has any feathery bits still attached. Lay out a large double layer of foil on a work surface, shiny side down. Rub the surface with butter.

Preheat the oven to 180°C (350°F/Gas 4). To make the stuffing, put the minced beef, sausage meat, parmesan, eggs and drained and squeezed-out bread in a bowl. Add the truffle butter, nutmeg, salt and pepper. Work the ingredients well together to mix. Lay the guinea fowl skin-side down on the foil and spread the filling over it, leaving the long sides free. Roll up compactly from one long side to the other. Salt and pepper the outside of the guinea fowl. Now fold the foil around it to seal completely.

Drizzle the olive oil over the bottom of a 22 x 30 cm (8½ x 12 inch) oven dish, put the guinea fowl on top and layer the bones around. Bake for about 40 minutes, then add the wine and cook for about 30 minutes more. Remove the foil from the guinea fowl and return to the oven for about 15 minutes, until it looks golden and the juices are bubbling. Remove the guinea fowl to a platter and keep warm. Discard the bones in the dish. Drizzle about 3 tablespoons of water into the dish and put on the stovetop to bubble up for a couple of minutes. Strain into a bowl. Cut the guinea fowl into 1 cm (½ inch) slices and serve with the hot pan juices.

— THE —

Dining Room

— MEAT —

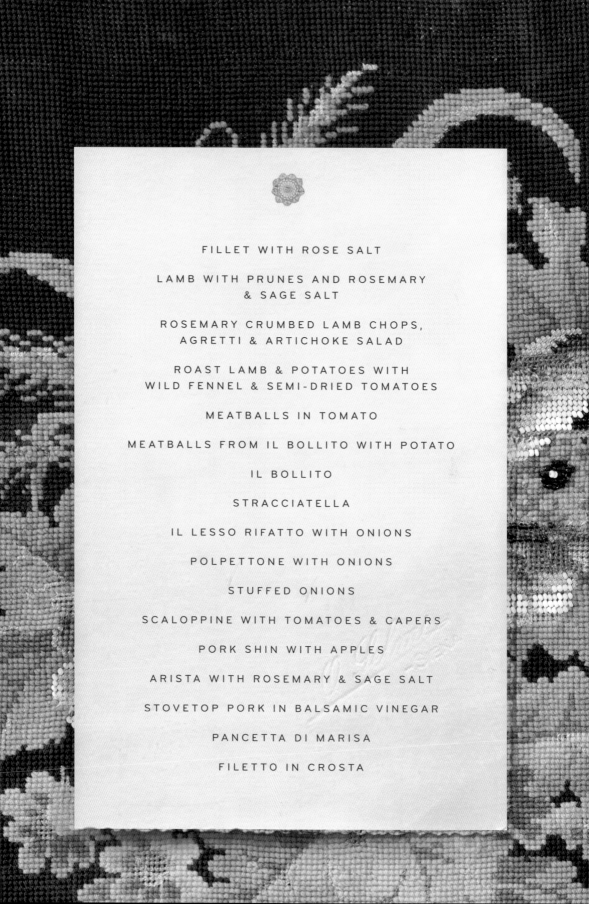

FILLET WITH ROSE SALT

LAMB WITH PRUNES AND ROSEMARY
& SAGE SALT

ROSEMARY CRUMBED LAMB CHOPS,
AGRETTI & ARTICHOKE SALAD

ROAST LAMB & POTATOES WITH
WILD FENNEL & SEMI-DRIED TOMATOES

MEATBALLS IN TOMATO

MEATBALLS FROM IL BOLLITO WITH POTATO

IL BOLLITO

STRACCIATELLA

IL LESSO RIFATTO WITH ONIONS

POLPETTONE WITH ONIONS

STUFFED ONIONS

SCALOPPINE WITH TOMATOES & CAPERS

PORK SHIN WITH APPLES

ARISTA WITH ROSEMARY & SAGE SALT

STOVETOP PORK IN BALSAMIC VINEGAR

PANCETTA DI MARISA

FILETTO IN CROSTA

SAPIENTE

WORDS/PAROLE

IT IS SAID THAT A SCATTERING
OF ROSE PETALS CAN HELP
IN UNLOCKING EMOTIONS

2 x 200 g (7 oz) BEEF
FILLET STEAKS, ABOUT
2 cm (¾ inch) THICK

1 TABLESPOON OLIVE OIL

ABOUT 30 g (1 oz) BUTTER

2 TABLESPOONS COGNAC

ROSE SALT (PAGE 24)

Serves 2

FILLET WITH ROSE SALT

This is subtle, elegant and quite gorgeous. You can taste the texture of the salt and see the rose petals. You will need a heavy-bottomed frying pan and a strong flame to give the steaks a good and golden crust. Serve with new potatoes boiled in their skins and then drizzled with olive oil and melted butter.

Bring the steaks to room temperature. Drizzle them with oil, then rub it into both sides. Heat the frying pan over a high flame to very hot. Add the steaks and cook for 2–3 minutes, until crusty and golden underneath. Turn over and cook until golden underneath once more. Add the butter to the pan, shaking it a little to distribute. Standing well back from the pan, add the cognac. It will probably catch fire and then burn out, so take care. Scatter some rose salt over each steak, add a grind or two of black pepper and remove from the heat. Let the steaks rest in the pan for 5 minutes in a warm place. Serve directly onto 2 warm plates, scraping the juices out on top and with an extra scattering of rose salt. Grind a little more pepper on if you like and serve immediately.

LAMB WITH PRUNES AND ROSEMARY & SAGE SALT

Beautiful, rich and deep. Just delicious. I love this with Sautéed artichokes & potatoes (page 107) and some crusty bread. Ask your butcher to debone the lamb or do it yourself if you know how.

Preheat the oven to 180°C (350°F/Gas 4). Drizzle 4 tablespoons of the olive oil onto a baking tin of about 22 x 30 cm (8½ x 12 inches). Lay 2 large sheets of foil on a work top, shiny side down and overlapping to give a larger surface. Rub with butter to grease well.

Rinse the lamb and pat dry with paper towels. Trim off any exaggerated fat, but leave most of it on for flavour and moistness. Put the lamb on a cutting board, skin side down and opened up like a book. Mix together the remaining 2 tablespoons of oil and the herbed salt, and massage half of it over the inside of the lamb. Line up the prunes in pairs like soldiers, running lengthways down the centre of the lamb. Wrap the sides of the lamb over to enclose the prunes. Tie up with kitchen string in a few places to hold the shape while cooking.

Rub the rest of the herby oil mix all over the outside of the lamb, then place it in the centre of the foil. Wrap up tightly, tucking in the sides. Put in the oiled tin and scatter the vegetables around (add the lamb bone, too, if you have it). Roast for about 40 minutes. Remove the foil from the lamb, scrape in any accumulated bits from the side of the tin and splash in the wine. Return to the oven for another 40 minutes or so, turning the lamb once or twice to brown all the sides and spooning the juices over. Add a little extra water if needed. To test if the lamb is done, prick it with a fork. The juices should run out, but not be pink.

Remove the lamb to a suitable dish. Cut away the string and leave it to rest for a bit while you make some gravy. Add the water to the baking tin and put it on the stovetop to bubble up and thicken a little. Scrape down any interesting bits from the sides of the tin into the juices.

Cut the meat into slices of about 1.5 cm (5⁄8 inch) and serve hot, with the juices spooned over.

6 TABLESPOONS OLIVE OIL

1 LEG OF LAMB (ABOUT 1.6 kg/ 3 lb 8 oz), DEBONED

2 TABLESPOONS ROSEMARY & SAGE SALT (PAGE 24)

12 PITTED PRUNES

2 MEDIUM CARROTS, PEELED AND CUT INTO LARGE CHUNKS

1 SMALL CELERY STICK

1 ONION, PEELED AND HALVED

185 ml (6 fl oz/¾ cup) WHITE WINE

ABOUT 125 ml (4 fl oz/ ½ cup) WATER

Serves 4–6

ROSEMARY CRUMBED LAMB CHOPS, AGRETTI & ARTICHOKE SALAD

THE LIST

6 NOT-TOO-THICK LAMB CHOPS (CUTLETS)

3 TABLESPOONS OLIVE OIL

2 GARLIC CLOVES, PEELED AND SQUASHED WITH THE FLAT OF A KNIFE

1 TABLESPOON CHOPPED ROSEMARY

1 EGG, BEATEN

ABOUT ½ teacup DRY BREADCRUMBS

LIGHT OLIVE OIL, FOR FRYING

Serves 3

Agretti and Artichoke salad (see page 202 for both) are refreshing partners for these fried lamb chops. Agretti is available in spring. It is very beautiful and elegant, like dark-green seaweedy spaghetti, and full of vitaminy goodness. Have your agretti cooked and salad things ready to assemble so when you have fried the chops you can serve it all immediately.

Rinse the lamb chops and pat dry with paper towels. On a board, pound the meat part with a meat mallet to flatten. Put the oil and garlic in a wide bowl with the rosemary, a sprinkling of salt and a few grinds of black pepper. Add the chops, turning them through to coat. Cover with plastic wrap and leave for an hour or so.

Put the egg in a wide bowl and the breadcrumbs on a flat plate. Shake the lamb chops out of the marinade and dip in the egg, coating all sides. Remove from the egg and shake off the excess, then press each one firmly into the breadcrumbs so they are coated on both sides. Finish breading all the lamb chops, keeping them on a plate until you are ready to fry them.

Heat enough light olive oil in a large frying pan to cover the bottom. Add the chops and fry until golden and crusty underneath. Turn them over and check that you have enough oil in the pan or the crumbs will burn. Fry until golden underneath once more and cooked through. Remove the lamb chops to a plate lined with paper towels to absorb any excess oil.

AGRETTI

THE
LIST

ABOUT 300 g (10½ oz) AGRETTI

2 TABLESPOONS OLIVE OIL

1 TABLESPOON LEMON JUICE

Serves 3

Cut away the bottom stems of the agretti, leaving just the algae-green parts on the top held together in clumps of two or three. You don't want individual strings. Rinse in a bowl of cold water and work through them, removing any unwanted things. You may feel like you are combing a mermaid's knotty hair. Bring a pot of salted water to the boil, add the agretti and boil for about 6 minutes or until tender. Drain, then drizzle with the olive oil and lemon juice, and give a grind of pepper and extra salt if necessary. Mix through.

ARTICHOKE SALAD

THE
LIST

1 SMALL LEMON, HALVED

1 ARTICHOKE

2 FISTFULS (ABOUT
40 g/1½ oz) VALERIANA
(LAMB'S LETTUCE)
OR WATERCRESS

2 TABLESPOONS OLIVE OIL

VANILLA SALT (PAGE 25)

Serves 3

Squeeze the juice from half the lemon into a bowl of water. Clean the artichoke, leaving a little of the stem. Cut away the top third or so of the bulb. Tear away as many leaves as necessary to get to the tender inner ones (you can nibble on the nibs of these). Halve it and scrape away the choke. Slice the halves into lengths of a couple of millimetres (fractions of an inch) each and drop these in the lemon water as you go so they don't go brown.

Put the valeriana in a bowl. Add the drained and patted-dry artichoke. Squeeze over the juice from the other lemon half and drizzle in the oil. Add a small scattering of vanilla salt, a few grinds of pepper and gently turn through. Serve next to the lamb and agretti, with a few extra grains of vanilla salt over the artichokes if you like.

ROAST LAMB & POTATOES WITH WILD FENNEL & SEMI-DRIED TOMATOES

1 SHOULDER OF LAMB, ABOUT 1.2 kg (2 lb 10 oz), WITH ONLY THE HEAVY FAT REMOVED

4–5 WILD FENNEL BRANCHES

6 TABLESPOONS OLIVE OIL

1 TEASPOON CRUSHED FENNEL SEEDS

3 GARLIC CLOVES, PEELED AND HALVED

5–6 THIN ROSEMARY SPRIGS

5–6 SAGE LEAVES

30 g (1 oz) PLUMP SEMI-DRIED TOMATOES, THICKLY SLICED

250 ml (9 fl oz/1 cup) WHITE WINE

750 g (1 lb 10 oz) POTATOES, SCRUBBED AND CUT INTO CHUNKS

Serves 4

You will need a few long fresh wild fennel branches to put in the bottom of the dish to perfume it all beautifully. I use a round dish, about 34 cm (13½ inches) in diameter, to cook this in. I like to serve it with a green salad (see page 102). If you can get crushed dried fennel flowers, use those instead of the fennel seeds here.

Preheat the oven to 200°C (400°F/Gas 6). Rinse the lamb and pat dry with paper towels. Cut 5 or 6 long slashes on the top. Make a bed of the fennel branches on the bottom of an oven dish and drizzle 4 tablespoons of olive oil over. Salt and pepper both sides of the lamb well and rub in the crushed fennel. Press a garlic half, a rosemary sprig, a sage leaf and a few slices of tomato into each slash. Put the lamb on top of the fennel branches and drizzle the remaining 2 tablespoons of olive oil over.

Roast until the top of the lamb is starting to change colour, about 20 minutes. Pour in the wine and add the potatoes around the lamb, turning them through the liquid. Lower the temperature to 180°C (350°F/Gas 4) and roast for 1 hour 15 minutes, turning the potatoes a few times. The lamb should be golden, nicely cooked and soft, and the potatoes should be golden brown. Serve the lamb cut in thick chunks, with the potatoes.

MEATBALLS
IN TOMATO

These are lovely served with mash, rice or some crushed boiled potatoes.

In a bowl, mix the minced beef, egg, parsley, mint, chilli and chopped garlic together and season with salt and pepper. Knead together well. Cover and put in the fridge for at least 30 minutes.

Heat 2 tablespoons of olive oil in a saucepan with the squashed garlic clove, and when it smells good add the tomatoes. Season with salt and pepper and simmer for about 10 minutes.

Shape the meat mixture into small balls the size of a walnut. Heat the extra 3 tablespoons of olive oil in a large non-stick frying pan and when hot, add the meatballs and fry gently until golden on all sides. Add the wine to the pan and let it reduce. Add the tomato sauce and the basil leaves, giving the pan a shake so it all mixes well. Cover and simmer for about 20 minutes. If it looks like it is drying out at any time, add a few drops of water. Taste for seasoning and serve warm.

300 g (10½ oz) MINCED (GROUND) BEEF

1 EGG, LIGHTLY BEATEN

1 TABLESPOON CHOPPED PARSLEY

1 TABLESPOON CHOPPED MINT

PINCH OF GROUND CHILLI

2 GARLIC CLOVES, PEELED, 1 CHOPPED AND 1 SQUASHED WITH THE FLAT OF A KNIFE

2 TABLESPOONS OLIVE OIL, PLUS 3 TABLESPOONS EXTRA, FOR FRYING

400 g (14 oz) TIN CHOPPED TOMATOES

125 ml (4 fl oz/½ cup) RED WINE

4 BASIL LEAVES, TORN

Serves 2–3

MEATBALLS FROM IL BOLLITO WITH POTATO

Here is a wonderful way that Wilma uses meat from a bollito. Actually, you could use any cooked meat to make these. Wilma serves them with Stracciatella (page 209), made from the bollito broth.

Boil the potatoes in salted water until soft. Drain and when cool enough to handle, peel and mash them. Chop up the meat finely, mix in the garlic and mash into the potato. Add the parsley, egg, parmesan, a good grating of nutmeg and a grind of pepper. There should be enough salt from the potatoes and bollito, but check just in case.

Shape into patties about 5 cm (2 inches) or so in diameter and 1 cm (½ inch) thick. Put the breadcrumbs on a plate, add the patties and turn to coat all sides, pressing the crumbs on with your fingers. Heat enough oil to cover the bottom of a non-stick frying pan. Fry the patties, in batches if necessary, until golden all over, turning them carefully with a fork so they don't break. Remove to a plate lined with paper towels to absorb excess oil. Give a small sprinkle of salt on top. These are good served with a squeeze of lemon juice or some herbed mayonnaise.

THE
LIST

320 g (11¼ oz) POTATOES, WASHED

300 g (10½ oz) MEAT FROM IL BOLLITO (PAGE 209)

1 GARLIC CLOVE, FINELY CHOPPED

1 TABLESPOON CHOPPED PARSLEY

1 EGG

2 TABLESPOONS GRATED PARMESAN

NUTMEG, FOR GRATING

ABOUT 4 TABLESPOONS DRY BREADCRUMBS

LIGHT OLIVE OIL, FOR FRYING

Serves 4–6

750 g (1 lb 10 oz) FAIRLY LEAN
BEEF, IN ONE OR TWO PIECES

2 CARROTS

1 CELERY STICK

1 LARGE ONION, PEELED

2 litres (70 fl oz/8 cups)
WATER

ABOUT 6 PEPPERCORNS

ABOUT 2 TEASPOONS SALT

Serves 4

IL BOLLITO

This is the base for many dishes. The boiled meat can be served with various sauces and marmalades, or turned into other dishes. The brodo (broth) can be used in a soup or is delicious to simply drink from a cup (brodo in tazza). This one is a simple brodo. You can add anything you like, such as a bay leaf, potato, fresh thyme, a whole tomato, depending on how you will be serving it. The meat needs a long time to cook and soften and you can make it in a pressure cooker if you prefer.

Rinse the meat and vegetables, then put in a pot. Cover with the water and add the peppercorns and salt. Bring to the boil. Skim off the scum that rises to the surface, lower the heat and put the lid on. Simmer for 2½–3 hours, until the meat is very tender when poked with a fork. Add extra water as it reduces. When it is ready, remove the meat to a board and strain the broth.

500 ml (17 fl oz/2 cups)
BRODO FROM IL BOLLITO
(SEE RECIPE ABOVE)

1 EGG

GRATED PARMESAN, AT LEAST
2 HEAPED TABLESPOONS

Serves 2

STRACCIATELLA

A much-appreciated soup among all generations, made with a deep tasty broth. It is often served to the convalescing, the young and the elderly. It needs that scattering of freshly grated parmesan flung on top when it's hot hot and then you are left to slurp away at this in your pretence of being ill. Stracci are rags, and that's what the strands of egg in the broth look like.

Pour the *brodo* into a shallow saucepan. Heat to a good boil and check the seasonings. Adjust if necessary. Whip the egg in a small bowl with a whisk. Pour into the hot broth, whisking so it gets the long *stracci*. Remove from the heat at once and divide between 2 bowls. Scatter a heaped tablespoon, if not two, of parmesan over each.

SAPIENTE
WORDS/PAROLE

SAME MEAT,
DIFFERENT GRAVY

IL LESSO RIFATTO
WITH ONIONS

This rifatto (re-done) style of cooking in Tuscany is common and takes very good care of leftovers. Here it is assumed you may have 500 g (1 lb 2 oz) leftover bollito meat. If not, you can just start from scratch of course. I like to add olives to this dish.

Chop up the meat into chunky slices. Heat the olive oil in a non-stick frying pan and sauté the onions until softened, nicely golden and a bit sticky. Add the garlic and when it smells good stir in the tomatoes. Add the chilli and oregano, and season with salt and pepper. Simmer for about 10 minutes. Add the meat, olives and tear in the basil. Turn through gently and cook until it is all harmonious, about 5 minutes. Serve with bread and a few torn basil leaves over the top.

500 g (1 lb 2 oz) MEAT FROM
IL BOLLITO (PAGE 209)

4 TABLESPOONS OLIVE OIL

2 LARGE RED ONIONS,
HALVED AND SLICED

1 GARLIC CLOVE, CHOPPED

400 g (14 oz) TIN
CHOPPED TOMATOES

GOOD PINCH OF GROUND CHILLI

½ TEASPOON DRIED OREGANO

1 HEAPED TABLESPOON
EACH OF PITTED GREEN
AND BLACK OLIVES

ABOUT 5 BASIL LEAVES, PLUS
A FEW EXTRA, TO SERVE

Serves 4

CAFFE
WILMA

IL CAFFE GIUSTO

—AM—
CAFFE LATTE
for the
morning
only

—AM—
CAPPUCCINO
only in the
morning

—PM—
CAFFE CORRETTO
for evening
or after lunch
or AM for some

—AM OR PM—
ESPRESSO
acceptable
anytime

—AM OR PM—
MACCHIATO
acceptable
anytime

POLPETTONE
WITH ONIONS

50 g (1¾ oz) CRUSTLESS
COUNTRY-STYLE BREAD

60 ml (2 fl oz/¼ cup) MILK

1 kg (2 lb 4 oz) LEAN BEEF,
FINELY MINCED (GROUND)

3 EGGS, LIGHTLY BEATEN

3 TABLESPOONS
GRATED PARMESAN

A GOOD GRATING OF NUTMEG

2 TABLESPOONS
CHOPPED PARSLEY

4 TABLESPOONS OLIVE OIL

125 ml (4 fl oz/½ cup)
WHITE WINE

250 ml (9 fl oz/1 cup) WATER

600 g (1 lb 5 oz) RED
ONIONS, SLICED

Serves 6–8

*This is Diana's recipe. She is a wonderful and elegant
nonna and cook. She asks for the mince to be passed
twice through the mincer as she likes it fine for this. Even
though there are eggs it's quite delicate and you have to
take care while turning it in the pan so it doesn't break.
If possible, use a large non-stick frying pan with fairly high
sides so that you can put a lid over the hill of meat in the
pan. Lovely with a dish of sliced tomatoes on the side.*

Break up the bread, put in a bowl and soak in the milk to
soften. Put the meat in another bowl and add the eggs,
parmesan, nutmeg and parsley, and season with salt and
pepper. Squeeze out the bread and add it to the bowl with
the meat. Mix together, then knead very well. Put in the
fridge for an hour or so.

Shape the mixture into a nice compact log that will
just fit in your pan. Heat the oil in the pan and gently lower
in the polpettone. Fry until golden underneath, then very
carefully roll to turn it using an egg lift or similar in both
hands. Fry until all the sides are golden and sealed, then
lower the heat and simmer for half an hour or so. Add
the wine and when most of it has evaporated add 125 ml
(4 fl oz/½ cup) of the water. Cover and simmer until the
meat is cooked through and clear juices seep out when
you prick it and press with a skewer, another half hour or
so. Carefully remove the polpettone to a serving platter to
rest, drizzled with some of the pan juices to keep it moist.

Add the onions to the juices remaining in the pan,
along with a little salt and pepper. Sauté until the onions
are golden, soft and a bit sticky. Add the remaining 125 ml
of water to loosen things up and continue to simmer. Keep
hot. Cut the meat into slices about 1.5 cm (⅝ inch), gently
supporting them with your hand as you go so they don't
collapse. Serve a couple of slices each, with a tablespoon
or so of hot onions spooned over.

STUFFED ONIONS

6 LARGE RED ONIONS,
200 g (7 oz) EACH

7 TABLESPOONS OLIVE OIL

550 g (1 lb 4 oz) MINCED
(GROUND) BEEF

4 HEAPED TABLESPOONS
CHOPPED PARSLEY

400 g (14 oz) TIN
CHOPPED TOMATOES

JUICE OF 1 LEMON

Serves 6–8

Delicious. Delicious. My mother's recipe. These little onion rolls look beautifully roasted in their oven dish, all top to tail and back to back.

Bring a large pot of unsalted water to the boil. Using a small sharp knife, carefully peel the skins off 5 of the onions, keeping them hinged at the bottom. Cut each onion with 1 slash lengthways, but just halfway through to the other side. This is to help the leaves loosen away during boiling. Boil until tender, about 15 minutes. Drain and cool a bit so you can handle them.

Peel and chop the remaining onion. Heat 3 tablespoons of the olive oil in a large non-stick frying pan. Add the chopped onion and sauté until softened and a bit golden. Add the minced beef and stir through, cooking until all the liquid has evaporated and the beef is cooked and golden brown. Season with salt and pepper, and stir in the parsley. Stir in half a cup of the tomatoes and cook for a couple of minutes. Remove from the heat.

Preheat the oven to 180°C (350°F/Gas 4). Have a large oven dish of about 34 x 24 cm (13½ x 9½ inches) ready. Sit at a table. Gently remove the onion leaves from the stems, carefully unfurling them so they don't tear. You need each leaf opened out as far as possible. The outer ones will of course be larger. Put about a tablespoon of mince towards one end of a leaf and roll up neatly and tightly. Fill and roll all the leaves, no matter how small they are, just add less filling to the little ones. Sit them in the dish, all tightly next to each other like seals on a beach. You won't be able to fill and roll the very inner leaves, but sit these in the dish as well.

Mix the remaining tomatoes and 4 tablespoons of olive oil with the lemon juice in a bowl and season with salt and pepper. Pour this mix over the onions and sprinkle a little salt over the onion tops sticking out above the sauce. Bake for about 1¼ hours, until roasty and the sauce is slightly thickened. Serve warm with bread. Even at room temperature these are great.

SCALOPPINE WITH TOMATOES & CAPERS

THE LIST

1 EGG

8 THIN PIECES (150 g/5½ oz IN TOTAL) BEEF CARPACCIO, ABOUT 10 x 8 cm (4 x 3¼ inches) EACH

ABOUT ½ teacup DRY BREADCRUMBS

4 TABLESPOONS OLIVE OIL

1 GARLIC CLOVE, PEELED AND SQUASHED WITH THE FLAT OF A KNIFE

1 cup CHOPPED TOMATOES (FROM A TIN)

3 OR 4 BASIL LEAVES

1 TABLESPOON CAPERS IN VINEGAR, DRAINED, CHOPPED QUITE FINE

Serves 4

I particularly love these very thin slices of meat, as they are buttery soft and just vanish in the mouth. Even though this takes a few minutes in the pan, you can make it a bit ahead of time. Leave in the pan, covered, then just warm up to serve, with a little water drizzled in to get it back to the right consistency.

Whip the egg in a wide bowl with a little salt and add the beef slices. Turn them over to coat. Put the breadcrumbs on a plate. Remove the meat one slice at a time from the egg, shake off the excess and pat both sides lightly in the crumbs to loosely cover.

Heat the oil in a large non-stick frying pan and add the garlic and crumbed meat slices. Fry quickly, until lightly golden underneath, then turn and fry the other side. Add the tomatoes to the pan, around and over the meat. Scatter a little salt over, tear in the basil, lower the heat and simmer for 8 minutes or so. Add the capers for the last couple of minutes. Turn off the heat, cover and leave for 5 minutes or so before serving. If not serving immediately, keep covered.

SAPIENTE
WORDS/PAROLE

A TAVOLA NON SI INVECCHIA
(At the table one doesn't get old)

1 kg (2 lb 4 oz) PORK SHIN

2 GARLIC CLOVES,
PEELED AND HALVED

8 SMALL TUFTS ROSEMARY

3 TABLESPOONS OLIVE OIL

2 BAY LEAVES

185 ml (6 fl oz/¾ cup)
WHITE WINE

2 (150 g/5½ oz EACH)
RED APPLES, UNPEELED

30 g (1 oz) BUTTER

3 SAGE LEAVES

4 JUNIPER BERRIES, SQUASHED

1 TABLESPOON COGNAC

ABOUT 60 ml (2 fl oz/
¼ cup) WATER

QUINCE JELLY
(PAGE 40), TO SERVE

Serves 2

PORK SHIN
WITH APPLES

Perfect with Quince jelly (page 40) and Marisa's potatoes with crumbs (page 106).

Preheat the oven to 180°C (350°F/Gas 4). Rinse the pork shin and pat dry with paper towels. Make 4 deep incisions in the meat and put 1 garlic half and 2 tufts of rosemary into each. Salt and pepper the outside of the pork well. Pour the olive oil over the bottom of a roasting pan, then add the pork and bay leaves. Roast until browned, about 40 minutes. Add the wine and roast for a further 1 hour 15 minutes, turning the pork a couple of times and adding a little water if necessary so it doesn't dry out.

Meanwhile, halve, core and slice the apple halves. Melt the butter in a frying pan and sauté the apple quickly with the sage, juniper and a little salt and pepper. Keep the slices intact, don't overcook them. Standing well back from the pan, add the cognac and let it evaporate. Take care when adding it as it may flame up.

Remove the pork to a board. Add the water to the roasting pan and let it bubble up on the stovetop to thicken. Carve slices of pork lengthways along the shin and put on a serving plate. Pour the sauce over and serve hot, with the apples and quince jelly on the side.

ARISTA WITH ROSEMARY & SAGE SALT

4 TABLESPOONS OLIVE OIL,
PLUS EXTRA, FOR SERVING

2½ TABLESPOONS ROSEMARY
& SAGE SALT (PAGE 24)

ABOUT 1.2 kg (2 lb 10 oz)
BONELESS AND RINDLESS
PORK LOIN, BUT WITH SOME FAT

125 ml (4 fl oz/½ cup)
WHITE WINE

Serves 6

I like to serve this with Marta's mum's fennel (page 103). Make sure you don't overcook the meat, it's nice when it is just slightly past the pink stage. Beyond this point it dries out easily. If you don't have any Rosemary & sage salt ready, you can make up a small amount now quickly. Leftovers are nice in panini the next day with some of the sauce and a little mustard.

Preheat the oven to 180°C (350°F/Gas 4). Combine 2 tablespoons of the oil with the herbed salt. Put the pork on a board. Spike a hole from one end to the other using the handle of a wooden spoon (not too thick), pushing it all the way through to create a tunnel. Use your fingers to stuff some of the herby oily mix in from both ends. Push it along with the handle of the wooden spoon to loosely fill the whole tunnel. This will give flavour inside and also look good when you slice the pork. Rub the rest of the herby oily mix all over the outside of the pork.

Lay a large sheet of foil on a work surface, shiny side down, and rub with butter. Put the pork in the middle and wrap up snugly. Drizzle the remaining 2 tablespoons of oil over a baking tin of about 25 x 18 cm (10 x 7 inches). Add the pork package and roast for about 30 minutes, by which time the juices around should be golden. Unwrap the pork, discard the foil and pour the wine around.

Return to the oven and roast for another 30 minutes or longer if necessary, until the pork is golden and the juices on the bottom of the dish are gooey. If the juices look like they are drying up during that time, dribble a little water into the tin. Pour in about 125 ml (4 fl oz/½ cup) water 10 minutes before the end of cooking. The pork is done when you press it with a fork and the juices run out clear, not pink. Rest it in the tin for 10 minutes or so, then remove to a board. Serve in thin slices with a little juice over and a little drizzling of olive oil.

To serve any leftovers, bring the meat to room temperature, then slice thinly and heat up only the juice. Pour the warm juice over the slices to serve.

STOVETOP PORK IN BALSAMIC VINEGAR

1.2 kg (2 lb 10 oz) BONELESS
AND RINDLESS PORK LOIN

4 TABLESPOONS OLIVE OIL

1 TEASPOON BLACK
PEPPERCORNS,
CRUSHED COARSELY

A CLUMP OF SAGE LEAVES
(ABOUT 6 LEAVES)

2 GARLIC CLOVES, PEELED
AND LIGHTLY SQUASHED
WITH THE FLAT OF A KNIFE

185 ml (6 fl oz/¾ cup)
BALSAMIC VINEGAR
(A REGULAR ONE WILL DO)

Serves 6

This is my friend Lisa's recipe. Everybody loves it when she makes it and they always say, 'There's hardly enough left for panini tomorrow!' And it's true, the leftovers and sauce stuffed into a panino the next day are exceptional. After the long cooking the pork is so tender that it's served more in pieces than slices. I love it with Salt & pepper potatoes with a trickle of buttermilk (page 110) and a green salad.

Tie up the pork or ask your butcher to tie it for you so it holds its shape neatly. Choose a pot that is not much larger than the pork so the sauce is not too shallow. Pour the oil in and heat well, then brown the pork on all sides, including each end. Salt the browned sides well and turn the pork around in the pot to seal in the salt.

Sprinkle the pepper over all the sides of the pork. Add the sage and garlic to the bottom of the pot and let them fizzle up and give out their flavours. Then, add the balsamic vinegar and let it bubble up. Cover with the lid and turn the heat down to an absolute minimum, hardly bubbling. Use a simmer mat if you have one. Simmer for 3½–4 hours, turning the pork over with tongs every half hour or so and adding just a little water if it looks too dry. The meat is ready when it comes away easily when you pull at it, and when the sauce is glossy and reduced.

Remove the pork to a chopping board. If the sauce is not abundant, add a little water to the pot and return it to the heat for it to bubble up. Remove the string from the meat, cut it up and serve with a good amount of sauce.

SAPIENTE

WORDS/PAROLE

AFTER DUSTING A COLOURFUL CARPET,
TAKE A COUPLE OF HEADS OF LETTUCE
AND RUB THEM ALL OVER THE CARPET
TO BRING OUT ITS COLOUR

THE
LIST

1 LONG FLAT PIECE OF
PORK BELLY WITH RIND
(ABOUT 1.5 kg/3 lb 5 oz)

1 TABLESPOON OLIVE OIL

3 TABLESPOONS ROSEMARY
& SAGE SALT (PAGE 24)

Serves many

PANCETTA DI MARISA

*A dream. Served warm on two thick slices of white
country-style bread it is wonderful. Bread in Tuscany is
unsalted and it works really well with a very flavourful, fatty
herby meat like this sandwiched in between. Serve it with
something that can stand up to it, like a radicchio salad
or a plate of cooked bitter greens.*

Preheat the oven to 200°C (400°F/Gas 6). Sit a wire rack
in a baking tin so the pork won't touch the bottom of the
tin and will crisp on all sides. Put the pork on a board, skin
side up, and prick the rind here and there with a metal
skewer or sharp pointed knife — it's quite tough but you
will manage. Turn the pork over and rub the olive oil into
the underside — this will also help the herbed salt stick.
Scatter 2 tablespoons of the herbed salt over evenly. Roll
up compactly and tie it with string in 3 or 4 places so it
holds its shape. With some oil still on your hands, rub the
skin all over, then rub the remaining herbed salt on.

Sit the pork on the rack in the tin and dribble a little
water into the tin. Roast in the oven for about 1 hour
45 minutes, lowering the temperature to 180°C (350°F/
Gas 4) for the last 30 minutes. Dribble in a little extra
water if the bottom of the tin is threatening to dry out at
any point. The outside of the pork will be deep golden and
crispy, and the inside soft (roast for an extra 10 minutes or
so, if necessary). Serve hot in slices, with bread.

FILETTO IN CROSTA

1 LOAF CIABATTA/BAGUETTE
TYPE BREAD

2 HEAPED TABLESPOONS
ROSEMARY & SAGE
SALT (PAGE 24)

4 TABLESPOONS OLIVE OIL

1 LONG PORK FILLET,
ABOUT 500 g (1 lb 2 oz)

8 SLICES OF LONG PANCETTA

Serves 4–6

I love this with Chilli & red pepper jam (page 37) and Salt & balsamic vinegar sautéed potatoes (page 111). It is best when the meat is just cooked, still a bit rose-coloured inside. Choose a loaf of bread of similar size to the pork.

Preheat the oven to 180°C (350°F/Gas 4). Halve the bread horizontally. If there is a lot of soft bread under the crusts, pluck out a little. Put most of the herbed salt on a board with 2 tablespoons of olive oil and rub all over the meat. Heat a non-stick frying pan to very hot. Sear the meat on all sides until it's a good colour, turning it carefully so you don't burn the herbs. Remove from the pan and nestle it in between the 2 halves of bread. Scatter with the remaining salt, then close it up like a sandwich and squash it down a bit. Trim away the ends of the bread so the loaf is the same length as the pork. Drape the pancetta over the top and sides. Tie with string in 4 or 5 places so the loaf will hold its shape.

Line a baking tray with baking paper. Drizzle another tablespoon of the olive oil onto the bottom. Sit the bread fillet on top and drizzle with the remaining tablespoon of olive oil. Roast for about 30 minutes or until it is golden and crusty on top, and when poked with a skewer the meat releases juices that are clear, not pink. Remove from the oven and sit for 10 minutes or so before slicing into chunky pieces. This is also good at room temperature.

WARRANTED
OF
SUPERIOR QUALITY

Chapter / Capitolo

Nº 9

Nine / Nove

— THE —

Dining Room

— FISH —

CHICKPEAS WITH PRAWNS

SEA BREAM WITH FENNEL & POTATOES

PERSICO WITH LEMON,
CAPERS & GREEN OLIVE MASH

PRAWNS WITH LARDO & INSALATA DI CAMPO

PEPPER PRAWNS

FISH WITH ESCAROLE, OLIVES & CAPERS

SCORFANO WITH ZUCCHINI, CHERRY
TOMATOES & OLIVES

BREADCRUMBED GRILLED CALAMARI WITH
TABASCO & THYME MAYONNAISE

FISH IN A BOTTLE

SALMON TROUT WITH TARRAGON
SALSA VERDE

GRILLED SCALLOPS
WITH TRUFFLE BUTTER

CHICKPEAS
WITH PRAWNS

This dish is a lovely, warming mix of rustic and elegant. Serve it with grilled bread rubbed with garlic and splashed with olive oil.

300 g (10½ oz) CHICKPEAS, SOAKED OVERNIGHT IN COLD WATER

3 GARLIC CLOVES, PEELED, 1 WHOLE AND 2 CHOPPED

A CLUMP OF SAGE

3 TABLESPOONS OLIVE OIL, PLUS EXTRA, FOR SERVING

400 g (14 oz) PEELED RAW MEDIUM PRAWNS (SHRIMP)

1 TABLESPOON CHOPPED ROSEMARY

400 g (14 oz) TIN WHOLE TOMATOES

2 GOOD PINCHES OF GROUND CHILLI

LARGE HANDFUL OF RUCOLA (ARUGULA)

Serves 4

Drain the chickpeas, put in a pot with the whole garlic clove and sage and cover with plenty of cold water. Bring to the boil. Skim any scum from the surface and cook until tender, about 50 minutes. They must surrender when you bite into them. Make sure you have enough water in the pot at the end, as you will need around 750 ml (26 fl oz/ 3 cups) of cooking liquid. Add salt only towards the end of cooking. Drain, keeping the liquid. Take out about a cup of the chickpeas and keep aside for now. Using a hand-held blender, purée the rest of the chickpeas with about 750 ml of the liquid to a smooth cream.

Heat 1 tablespoon of oil in a non-stick frying pan and add the prawns and rosemary. Sauté on a strong heat until a bit golden, just a couple of minutes. Scatter a little salt and pepper over, remove to a plate and keep warm.

Add the remaining 2 tablespoons of oil and the chopped garlic to the pan. When the garlic starts to smell good add the tomatoes and chilli. Season with salt and a little pepper. Cook over high heat for about 5 minutes, breaking up the tomatoes into big chunks with a wooden spoon. Tip into the chickpea purée and simmer together for 5 minutes to meld the flavours.

Spoon the soup into 4 warm wide bowls and divide the prawns among them. Add a few whole chickpeas and top each with a small handful of rucola. Drizzle with olive oil, give a grind of pepper and serve.

SEA BREAM WITH FENNEL & POTATOES

THE
········· LIST ·········

550 g (1 lb 4 oz)
POTATOES, WASHED

2 TABLESPOONS OR
SO FENNEL SEEDS

2 TABLESPOONS
CHOPPED PARSLEY

3 GARLIC CLOVES, PEELED,
1 CHOPPED AND 2 WHOLE

2 SMALL SEA BREAM (ORATA),
ABOUT 350 g (12 oz) EACH,
GUTTED AND SCALED
FOR OVEN ROASTING

2 CLUMPS OF PARSLEY,
WITH STALKS

A LITTLE COARSE SALT

4 TABLESPOONS OLIVE OIL,
PLUS EXTRA, FOR SERVING

2 TABLESPOONS GRATED
MATURE PECORINO
(OR PARMESAN)

125 ml (4 fl oz/½ cup)
WHITE WINE

Serves 2

The fennel here is a beauty. For the sea bream, I like them rounded and small. When I buy fish in Italy they always ask if I want it cleaned for grilling or oven roasting. I like this, that they bother to ask how you will be cooking your fish. I often ask them how to cook it, and for the recipe! Any small whole fish is of course suitable.

Cook the potatoes in their skins in boiling salted water until they are soft all the way through, but not falling apart. Drain and when cool enough to handle, peel them. Slice into rounds of about 1 cm (½ inch).

Preheat the oven to 180°C (350°F/Gas 4). Chop up the fennel seeds, so that some are coarse and some dust. Use a pestle and mortar if you prefer. Keep aside. On a small plate mix the chopped parsley and chopped garlic.

Rinse the fish and wipe with paper towels. Into the cavity of each put a whole garlic clove, a clump of parsley and a sprinkling of coarse salt. Drizzle 2 tablespoons of olive oil into an oven dish that will hold the fish fairly compactly. Lay the potatoes over the oil. Scatter a tablespoon of the garlic parsley, a tablespoon of the pecorino and a tablespoon of the fennel over. Salt and pepper the outside of each fish, then lay them on top. Scatter the rest of the garlic parsley, pecorino and fennel over. Drizzle the last 2 tablespoons of oil over and pour the wine around too. Roast, uncovered, for about 30 minutes or until the fish are roasty looking on top and when you pierce one in the very middle with a knife it comes out hot.

Serve the potatoes with the fish, and a plate on the side to fillet the fish on. Drizzle a little olive oil over the fish on your plate and give a grinding of black pepper.

PERSICO WITH LEMON, CAPERS & GREEN OLIVE MASH

1 LEMON, RINSED AND SCRUBBED

700 g (1 lb 9 oz) POTATOES, SCRUBBED

185 ml (6 fl oz/¾ cup) WARM MILK

50 g (1¾ oz) BUTTER

70 g (2½ oz) PITTED GREEN OLIVES, HALVED OR QUARTERED IF LARGE

2 TABLESPOONS OLIVE OIL

2 GARLIC CLOVES, PEELED AND LIGHTLY SQUASHED WITH THE FLAT OF A KNIFE

4 PERSICO (PERCH) FILLETS, ABOUT 170 g (5¾ oz) EACH

1 HEAPED TABLESPOON SMALL CAPERS IN VINEGAR, DRAINED

60 ml (2 fl oz/¼ cup) WATER

Serves 4

The mash is quite abundant, but there is never really enough mash, is there?

Grate about a teaspoon of rind from the yellow part of the lemon. Keep aside. Cut 4 slices of lemon, a few millimetres (fractions of an inch) thick, from one end and then squeeze the juice from what's left. Keep aside.

Meanwhile, boil the potatoes in their skins in boiling salted water until they are soft all the way through when you pierce them with a fork. Drain and when cool enough to handle, peel and then put back in the pot. Mash them, adding the lemon rind. Add the warm milk and butter and turn through well. Stir in the olives and season with salt and pepper. Keep warm.

Heat the oil in a large non-stick frying pan, add the garlic and fish fillets and sauté over medium heat until they are a bit golden underneath. Turn them over, add the lemon slices to the pan and fry until the fish is golden underneath once more. Turn the lemon slices too, so they are golden and caramel on each side. Season with salt and pepper, add the lemon juice and scatter the capers over the fish. Put the lid on and simmer for a minute more, until the lemon juice is a syrupy sauce and the fish is cooked through. Remove the fish and lemon slices to warm serving plates. Add the water to the pan and return to the heat. Simmer, uncovered, to reduce a little. Pour over the fish and serve with an extra grind of pepper and a pile of mash on the side.

1 GARLIC CLOVE, PEELED
AND SQUASHED WITH
THE FLAT OF A KNIFE

2 TABLESPOONS OLIVE OIL

½ TABLESPOON
BALSAMIC VINEGAR

½ TABLESPOON LEMON JUICE

1 LARGE MURCOTT MANDARIN

2 HANDFULS
INSALATA DI CAMPO/
MISTICANZA

6 RAW LARGE PRAWNS
(SHRIMP), UNPEELED

6 THIN SLICES OF LARDO

1½ TABLESPOONS OLIVE OIL

HANDFUL OF THYME SPRIGS,
PLUS EXTRA, TO SERVE,
IF YOU LIKE

2 TABLESPOONS COGNAC

Serves 2

PRAWNS WITH LARDO
& INSALATA DI CAMPO

Here, prawns are wrapped in thin, pure white slices of cured pork fat (lardo) and sautéed to give a light savoury crust. Lardo di Colonnata was originally a humble food but today it is a prized ingredient in Tuscany. Thinly sliced pancetta could be substituted here. Insalata di campo are wild salad leaves gathered from the fields and they are bitter, beautiful and quite special.

Make the salad dressing. Put the garlic in a small bowl, add the olive oil, balsamic vinegar and lemon juice, and season with salt and pepper. Peel the mandarin and cut it crossways into 6 slices. Add to the dressing. If the salad leaves are very big, tear them up into good-sized pieces.

Peel the prawns, leaving the heads and tails on. Devein them, then rinse and pat dry with paper towels. Wrap a piece of lardo around the body of each prawn. The loose end will stick. Heat the olive oil in a large non-stick frying pan. Carefully add the prawns in a single layer and sauté over a strong heat until golden and crusty underneath. Using a pair of tongs, gently turn them over. Add the thyme to the bottom of the pan and sprinkle a little salt and pepper over the prawns. The lardo is well seasoned but you will still need a little. Sauté until golden underneath once more. Standing well back, add the cognac to the pan. It will probably flame up, so take care. When it has burnt out, remove the pan from the heat.

Divide the salad leaves between 2 plates. Drizzle the dressing over the leaves and add the mandarin slices around each salad. Put 3 prawns on each plate and drizzle the pan juices over. Give an extra grind of black pepper and serve at once.

SAPIENTE

WORDS/PAROLE

PEPPERCORNS CAN BE SEWN
INTO LINEN SACHETS AND
KEPT IN POCKETS OF FUR OR
WOOLLEN COATS TO KEEP
INSECTS AWAY. THEY CAN ALSO
BE PUT IN JARS OF LENTILS OR
BEANS TO DISTRACT INSECTS

THE
LIST

PEPPER PRAWNS

10 RAW LARGE PRAWNS
(SHRIMP), UNPEELED

1 GENEROUS TEASPOON
PINK PEPPERCORNS

1 GENEROUS TEASPOON
BLACK PEPPERCORNS

3 TABLESPOONS OLIVE OIL

1½ TABLESPOONS DRY
BREADCRUMBS

LEMON WEDGES, TO SERVE

Serves 2

This is indeed peppery and great. It is good with a clean-tasting green salad and bread.

Remove the heads from the prawns, leaving the shells and tails intact. Split open down the back to butterfly them, then devein. Rinse and pat dry with paper towels. Sprinkle some salt on the cut side of each prawn.

In a mortar, crush the pink and black peppercorns with a pestle to break up roughly. Each should be smashed, some smaller than others. Pour 2 tablespoons of olive oil into an ovenproof dish large enough to take the prawns in a single layer. Scatter the breadcrumbs over the bottom, then add the prawns. Scatter the crushed pepper over the prawns. Turn each one over, wiping them in the oil and breadcrumbs, then turn cut side up again and leave for half an hour or so.

Preheat the oven grill to hot. Drizzle the remaining tablespoon of oil over the prawns and grill them until opaque and a bit golden here and there, but not dried out, about 10 minutes. Serve with a squeeze of lemon juice.

FISH WITH ESCAROLE, OLIVES & CAPERS

◇◇

THE
LIST

1 WHOLE ESCAROLE
(CURLY ENDIVE/CHICORY),
ABOUT 560 g (1 lb 4¼ oz)

5 TABLESPOONS OLIVE OIL,
PLUS EXTRA, FOR SERVING

2 GARLIC CLOVES, PEELED
AND SQUASHED WITH
THE FLAT OF A KNIFE

3 ANCHOVY FILLETS, DRAINED

1 HEAPED TABLESPOON SMALL
CAPERS IN VINEGAR, DRAINED

ABOUT 12 BLACK OLIVES
(TAGGIASCHE ARE GOOD)

ABOUT 3 TABLESPOONS FLOUR

4 FIRM WHITE FISH FILLETS,
ABOUT 170 g (5¾ oz) EACH

4 SAGE LEAVES

ABOUT 1 TABLESPOON
CHOPPED PARSLEY

60 ml (2 fl oz/¼ cup)
WHITE WINE

Serves 4

The escarole is also great to serve with Il bollito (page 209). Try to get a compact escarole that looks like it has been to a neat hairdresser, rather than a wild one.

Rinse the escarole and trim away the bottom. Divide in half lengthways and then in half crossways, so you have nice thick chunks. Heat 2 tablespoons of the olive oil in a large non-stick frying pan with 1 garlic clove and the anchovies, mashing these in with a wooden spoon until they break up and melt into the oil. Add the escarole and cook until wilted, turning it with a pair of tongs so it picks up the flavours in the pan. Add the capers and olives, and season with pepper and a little salt (remember you have anchovies in the sauce). Cook, stirring, on a good heat until much of the water from the escarole has evaporated and you have a thick, chunky heap in the pan, not soggy. Taste for seasoning, remove to a dish and keep warm.

Wipe out the pan with paper towels, then heat the remaining 3 tablespoons of olive oil. Pat a little flour over both sides of the fish, shaking off the excess. Fry the fish until golden underneath. Turn them over using tongs, add the sage and remaining garlic and fry until the fish is golden underneath once more. Season with salt and pepper and add the wine to the pan. Cook until the wine has mostly evaporated, then scatter the parsley over. Serve on a heap of escarole, drizzled with a little extra olive oil and seasoned with lots of black pepper.

INSIDE A LADY'S HANDBAG IS A COMB,
A NEEDLE AND THREAD, A PLASTER,
A NATURAL REMEDY, A LIPSTICK —
ANYTHING SHE, A CHILD OR A MAN MAY
NEED. IT'S ALL THERE AT THE SAME TIME,
TO COVER ALL OF HER CONCERNS

SCORFANO WITH ZUCCHINI, CHERRY TOMATOES & OLIVES

THE LIST

4 TABLESPOONS OLIVE OIL, PLUS EXTRA, FOR SERVING

300 g (10½ oz) SMALL ZUCCHINI (COURGETTES), RINSED AND SLICED QUITE THINLY

4 FILLETS (ABOUT 600 g/ 1 lb 5 oz IN TOTAL) SCORFANO (SCORPION FISH)

200 g (7 oz) CHERRY TOMATOES ON STALKS, BIG ONES CAN BE HALVED

1 HEAPED TABLESPOON CHOPPED PARSLEY

6 BASIL LEAVES

125 ml (4 fl oz/½ cup) WHITE WINE

20 OR SO WHOLE BLACK OLIVES

Serves 4

This is lovely and has the accessories (zucchini and tomatoes) included so you don't have to serve any vegetables on the side. All you need to do is the preparation, then it just does its own thing in the oven. You could nip out to the shops — all you need is someone to take it out of the oven for you when the buzzer goes. You can use any delicate white-fleshed fish fillets here.

Preheat the oven to 180°C (350°F/Gas 4). I use a rectangular oven dish, about 22 x 30 cm (8½ x 12 inches). Drizzle 2 tablespoons of the olive oil into the dish and scatter the zucchini over. Salt and pepper both sides of the fish and lay them on the zucchini. Add the tomatoes and scatter in the parsley and torn basil leaves. Add a little salt and pepper over the tomatoes and zucchini. Pour the wine around and throw the olives in. Drizzle the remaining 2 tablespoons of olive oil over. Put in the oven for about 30–40 minutes, until it's all roasty looking. Serve with a little extra olive oil drizzled over the top.

BREADCRUMBED GRILLED CALAMARI WITH TABASCO & THYME MAYONNAISE

400 g (14 oz) SMALL CALAMARI
(SQUID) (ABOUT 6)

2 TABLESPOONS DRY
BREADCRUMBS

2 TABLESPOONS
CHOPPED PARSLEY

1 TEASPOON
CHOPPED THYME

3 TABLESPOONS
OLIVE OIL

LEMON WEDGES,
TO SERVE

TABASCO & THYME
MAYONNAISE (PAGE 252)

Serves 2

This can be served as an antipasto or light lunch. Make a couple of crostini from the calamari wings (see below). This is the kind of thing my mother-in-law, Wilma, always does and it adds an extra treat to the meal.

Clean the calamari. This can be done ahead of time and they can be kept them in the fridge until you are ready to eat. Remove the wings and save them for a crostino topping (below). Cut the bodies of the calamari into thick rings of about 3 cm (1¼ inches). Leave the tentacles whole unless they are large, in which case halve them. Put the breadcrumbs, parsley and thyme on a plate and mix with some salt and pepper.

Preheat the oven grill to the highest temperature. Add the calamari to the crumb mixture and toss them about so they are coated in crumbs. Drizzle 2 tablespoons of olive oil over a non-stick baking dish where the calamari will fit compactly but in a single layer, about 18 x 25 cm (7 x 10 inches). Add the calamari and drizzle the remaining 1 tablespoon of olive oil over the top. Place under the grill and cook for about 10 minutes or until the calamari are cooked and the breadcrumbs on the bottom of the dish are crusty brown. Serve warm or at room temperature, with lemon wedges and Tabasco & thyme mayonnaise.

For the crostino, chop up the calamari wings and sauté in a small frying pan with some olive oil until golden. Add some chopped garlic, a little salt and black pepper and a pinch of ground chilli and sauté for a couple of minutes more. Grill 2 small slices of bread, top with the calamari wings and drizzle with olive oil.

SAPIENTE
WORDS/PAROLE

TABASCO &
THYME MAYONNAISE

THE
LIST

150 ml (5 fl oz) LIGHT OLIVE OIL

150 ml (5 fl oz) SUNFLOWER OIL

1 GARLIC CLOVE, PEELED
AND SQUASHED WITH
THE FLAT OF A KNIFE

2 EGG YOLKS

2 TABLESPOONS FRESHLY
SQUEEZED LEMON JUICE

1 TEASPOON DIJON MUSTARD

½ TEASPOON CHOPPED THYME

½ TEASPOON CHOPPED PARSLEY

½–1 TEASPOON TABASCO
SAUCE, TO TASTE

Makes 1¼ cups

Combine the olive oil, sunflower oil and garlic in a bowl
and leave for 15 minutes or so for the garlic to flavour the
oils. Put the egg yolks in a larger bowl and beat with a
whisk until creamy. Remove the garlic clove from the oil
and whisk a drop or two of the oil into the egg yolks. When
that is amalgamated, whisk in a few drops more. Continue
like this until you can see that the emulsion is thickening,
then you can gradually increase the rate at which you
whisk in the oil. The mixture should become thicker as
you go and be quite stiff by the time all the oil has been
incorporated. Stir in the lemon juice and mustard. Fold
the thyme and parsley through and add salt and freshly
ground black pepper to taste. Stir in Tabasco, to taste.

4 FIRM WHITE FISH FILLETS
(SUCH AS PERCH OR COD),
ABOUT 150 g (5½ oz) EACH

2 SMALL BUNCHES THYME

2 SMALL BUNCHES
PARSLEY, WITH STALKS

10 BLACK PEPPERCORNS

2 TABLESPOONS OLIVE OIL

2 GARLIC CLOVES, PEELED
AND SQUASHED WITH
THE FLAT OF A KNIFE

DRESSING

4 TABLESPOONS OLIVE OIL

JUICE OF 1 LEMON

1 GARLIC CLOVE, PEELED
AND SQUASHED WITH
THE FLAT OF A KNIFE

———

Serves 4

FISH IN A BOTTLE

✕✕✕✕✕✕✕✕✕✕✕✕✕✕✕✕✕✕✕✕✕✕✕✕✕✕✕✕✕✕✕✕✕✕

This is unbelievable. There is no smell of fish in the kitchen or lingering in the house. I imagine a good housewife making this at the same time as she boils other preserves in a water bath. That way she would have jams preserved for months ahead and what's more, lunch ready. The house would be smelling of washed sheets and fresh flowers, and she'd be looking like she's come from the day spa.

You will need 2 low and wide preserving jars that have good watertight lids. Into each, put 2 fish fillets, a bunch of thyme and parsley in between and over, some salt, peppercorns, a tablespoon of olive oil and a garlic clove. Close and seal the jars well. Place the jars in a wide pot and add enough water to cover at least the necks of the jars (make sure the water won't be able to enter the jars). Take the jars out now and bring the water to the boil. Lower the jars carefully into the boiling water, so they're not touching, and return to the boil. Simmer until the fish turns white, 20–30 minutes. Remove the jars from the bath and cool a little before opening.

While the fish is cooking make the dressing. Put the olive oil and lemon juice with some salt and pepper in a small bowl and whip until it has thickened a bit. Add the garlic clove and leave for the flavours to mingle. Serve a fish fillet per plate with some dressing spooned over. This is so simple, it doesn't need anything else. The little broth collected in the bottles after steaming can be used to dress rice as a first course.

SALMON TROUT WITH TARRAGON SALSA VERDE

THE

LIST

250 ml (9 fl oz/1 cup) WATER

125 ml (4 fl oz/½ cup)
WHITE WINE

1 SMALL WHITE ONION,
PEELED AND HALVED

1 SMALL CELERY STICK

SMALL BUNCH OF PARSLEY

A FEW BLACK PEPPERCORNS

1 SALMON TROUT
(OCEAN TROUT),
ABOUT 850 g (1 lb 14 oz),
FILLETED WITH SKIN LEFT ON

SALSA VERDE (PAGE 18)

Serves 2

Lovely, fresh, summery and easy. Serve with sliced new potatoes boiled in their skins. Don't throw the broth away. Keep it to make a fish risotto later (see below).

Choose a nice wide pot where the fish fillets won't be compromised. Add the water, wine, onion, celery, parsley bunch, peppercorns and a good pinch of salt and bring to the boil. Clean the fish fillets and remove any bones. Add the fish to the broth, skin side down, cover and simmer for 10 minutes or so. Make sure you splash some of the liquid over the top of the fish. Remove from the heat and leave for about 5 minutes, then carefully remove each fillet to a plate. Keep the broth to make risotto (see below). Put another plate on top, upside down, and flip it over so it holds the fish, skin side up. Peel the skin away. Flip with the plate-over method once more to have the best side up for presentation. Serve with salsa verde on the side, and boiled new potatoes.

For the risotto, chop ½ small white onion and sauté in 2 tablespoons olive oil in a wide pan. Add 160 g (5½ oz) arborio or carnaroli rice (or 4 fistfuls per person, so 8 here). Stir for a couple of minutes, then add some hot water. When it's absorbed, stir in the strained leftover fish broth and simmer for 20 minutes, until the rice is tender. To finish, add a tablespoon of olive oil and 2 tablespoons of grated parmesan. Turn through some chopped parsley or any other herb you like. Serve with extra grated parmesan and a grinding of black pepper. Serves 2

SAPIENTE
WORDS/PAROLE

TO ENSURE YOUR PEARLS STAY
BEAUTIFUL, KEEP THEM IMMERSED
IN MAGNESIUM POWDER

GRILLED
SCALLOPS WITH
TRUFFLE BUTTER

THE
LIST

6 GOOD-LOOKING SCALLOPS
IN THEIR SHELLS

6 HEAPED TEASPOONS
TRUFFLE BUTTER (PAGE 19)

ABOUT 1 TABLESPOON
DRY BREADCRUMBS

Serves 2

*One of the easiest recipes I know, and also one
of the most elegant.*

Detach the scallops with their coral from their shells
and rinse and pat dry both. Salt and pepper both sides
of the scallops, then replace them in their shells. Put the
shells on a baking tray.

Preheat the oven grill to high. Spoon 1 heaped
teaspoonful of truffle butter onto each scallop and
sprinkle lightly with breadcrumbs. Put under the grill for
a couple of minutes, until the butter has melted and
the scallops are just cooked through and nicely golden.
Serve at once.

— THE —

Sugar Bin

RASPBERRY CARAMEL PASTRIES WITH
CREME FRAICHE

BRUTTI MA BUONI

LEONTINE'S APPLE CAKE

FRUIT SALAD TART

FILOMENA'S APPLE CAKE

RADICCHIO CAKE WITH WHITE
CHOCOLATE ICING

TORTA TARTUFATA

CHOCOLATE SPREAD

LEMON VERBENA PEACHES & CREAM

ROSE BISCUITS

LEMON BISCUITS WITH VIOLETS

LAVENDER BISCUITS

CROSTATA DI CREMA

CROSTATA WITH PEACH JAM

NONNA'S EGG WHITE CAKE & CANTUCCINI

TORTA CAMPAGNOLA

TORTA MIMOSA

GRANNY JOY'S MARMALADE CAKE

NONNA'S DOLCE DI MARIE

LEMON PIE

BACI DI DAMA

RASPBERRY CARAMEL PASTRIES WITH CREME FRAICHE

THE
————— LIST —————

PASTRY
60 g (2¼ oz) BUTTER

60 g (2¼ oz) FLOUR

20 g (¾ oz) SUGAR

1 TABLESPOON COLD WATER

CARAMEL SAUCE
50 g (1¾ oz) BUTTER

½ TEASPOON VANILLA EXTRACT

140 g (5 oz/⅔ cup) SUGAR

125 ml (4 fl oz/½ cup)
POURING (WHIPPING) CREAM

TO ASSEMBLE
ABOUT 8 HEAPED TEASPOONS
CREME FRAICHE, NOT
ICE-COLD FROM THE FRIDGE

250 g (9 oz/2 cups) RASPBERRIES,
AT ROOM TEMPERATURE

ICING (CONFECTIONERS')
SUGAR, FOR DUSTING

————

Makes 8

I love this not-too-sweet combination. You can break up the steps and make the biscuits and caramel in advance. The caramel should be taken to a handsome deep-cognac colour and you can test when it is ready by putting a drop on a white surface. If it looks too light, carry on cooking but take care as it can burn in a second. This makes eight whispers of a dessert — you may hardly realise you've had dessert.

To make the pastry, cut up the butter into a bowl, then add the flour, sugar and a pinch of salt and crumble with your fingers to make crumbs. Don't overwork the mixture or it will compromise the biscuit texture. Keep the movements of your fingers light and quick. Work in the water to form a soft dough. Gather it into a ball, cover with plastic wrap and put in the fridge to rest for at least half an hour.

Preheat the oven to 180°C (350°F/Gas 4). Line a baking tray with baking paper. Remove the pastry from the fridge. Fold one end over the other a few times, pressing down to give a few layers. Divide the pastry into 8 portions and use your fingers to flatten each into a disc of 7–8 cm (2¾–3¼ inches) in diameter. Put them on the prepared tray and bake for about 12 minutes or until pale gold but not too crisp. Remove to cool. They are fragile, so take care.

For the caramel sauce, gently heat the butter, vanilla and sugar together in a heavy-bottomed saucepan until melted. Continue cooking over low heat until it is a good amber colour. Meanwhile, heat the cream in a separate small saucepan. When the caramel is a good colour, carefully whisk in the cream, bit by bit. It will bubble up so take care. Continue cooking for a minute or so more to ensure that it is smooth and there are no lumps. You may need to give it a good whisk to make it smooth again. If the caramel gets too dark at any point, plunge the pan into a bowl of cold water to stop it cooking further. Whisk as it cools. Keep, covered, until ready to use. It will be nice and thick, and will cling to your pastry discs.

Take quite a heaped teaspoon of caramel and edge it off onto a pastry disc using another teaspoon. It will spread a bit and settle in. Using the same teaspoon technique, edge a teaspoon or so of crème fraîche over the middle of the caramel and pat out a bit with the spoon to distribute evenly. Set 3 or 4 raspberries on top so it looks a bit queen of heart-ish, and put a couple of raspberries on the side. Continue with the other plates in the same way. Shake a little icing sugar over each. You can then turn the raspberries over to see their colour. Serve the tarts with a spoon and fork.

BRUTTI MA BUONI

THE

--------- LIST ---------

100 g (3½ oz) BLANCHED ALMONDS

1 EGG, SEPARATED

120 g (4¼ oz) SUGAR

90 g (3¼ oz) BUTTER, SOFTENED

1 TEASPOON VANILLA EXTRACT

175 g (6 oz) PLAIN (ALL-PURPOSE) FLOUR

1 TEASPOON GROUND CINNAMON

Makes about 28

Ugly but good, as the name says. These are often served with coffee, but can be served on their own. I love them with the Coffee & cassia ice cream (page 314).

Preheat the oven to 180°C (350°F/Gas 4) and line 2 baking trays with baking paper. Grind the almonds coarsely so you have a few bits in your biscuits. Use electric beaters to whip the egg white and half the sugar to soft peaks in a small bowl first so you don't have to wash the beaters. Keep aside or in the fridge but don't leave it too long or it will deflate.

Use the electric beaters to whip the butter and the rest of the sugar together until creamy. Add the egg yolk and vanilla, then add the flour, cinnamon, almonds and a pinch of salt and mix in with a wooden spoon. Incorporate the beaten egg white.

Grab chunks of dough smaller than an apricot and rest them on the prepared trays in rows. Bake for about 12 minutes, until pale golden and firm. Cool on the trays and store in a pretty tin.

LEONTINE'S APPLE CAKE

125 g (4½ oz) BUTTER, SOFTENED

250 g (9 oz) RAW
(DEMERARA) SUGAR

1 EGG

250 g (9 oz/1²/₃ cups) PLAIN
(ALL-PURPOSE) FLOUR

½ TEASPOON
BAKING POWDER

½ TEASPOON
VANILLA EXTRACT

4 COOKING APPLES
(SUCH AS RENNET OR
GOLDEN DELICIOUS),
ABOUT 750 g (1 lb 10 oz) IN TOTAL

POURING (WHIPPING)
CREAM, FOR SERVING

PINCH OF GROUND
CINNAMON

ICING (CONFECTIONERS') SUGAR,
FOR DUSTING

*Makes a 24 cm
(9½ inch) cake*

This is my friend Leontine's cake — everyone is happy when she turns up with it. The crust is great and it lasts well (if there is any left over, that is). It is great alone or with cinnamon cream.

Preheat the oven to 170°C (325°F/Gas 3). Butter and flour a round 24 cm (9½ inch) springform cake tin.

Using electric beaters, cream the butter and sugar in a bowl and then beat in the egg. Mix in the flour, baking powder and vanilla, switching to mix with your hands when it gets too stiff. Knead briefly to incorporate everything.

Put about two-thirds of the dough in the prepared tin. Press it firmly over the bottom and two-thirds of the way up the side. Peel the apples, quarter and core them and chop into pieces of about 2 cm (¾ inch). Put the apples over the crust and even them out, checking there are no gaps. Crumble the rest of the pastry evenly over the apples in nice big crumbly bits. Bake for 55–60 minutes or until the pastry is golden and firm. Towards the end, cover the top with a sheet of foil if it looks like over-browning. Remove from the oven and cool.

Whip the cream to soft peaks, scattering in the cinnamon. Dust the cake with icing sugar and serve with the cinnamon cream.

PASTRY

125 g (4½ oz) BUTTER, SOFTENED

210 g (7½ oz) RAW
(DEMERARA) SUGAR

1 EGG

½ TEASPOON VANILLA EXTRACT

250 g (9 oz/1⅔ cups) PLAIN
(ALL-PURPOSE) FLOUR

½ TEASPOON BAKING POWDER

FILLING

500 g (1 lb 2 oz/ABOUT 4 cups)
ASSORTED FRUIT, SUCH AS
PEACHES, PEARS, PLUMS,
CHERRIES, STRAWBERRIES,
BLUEBERRIES, NECTARINES

2 TABLESPOONS RAW
(DEMERARA) SUGAR

ICING (CONFECTIONERS')
SUGAR, FOR DUSTING

WHIPPED CREAM, TO SERVE,
IF YOU LIKE

*Makes a 24 cm
(9½ inch) cake
+ 10 biscuits*

FRUIT SALAD TART

*Here is a lovely fruit tart that is easy to make, and you'll
even have pastry left over to make some sweet and
crunchy biscuits (see below).*

Preheat the oven to 180°C (350°F/Gas 4). Butter and flour
a round 24 cm (9½ inch) springform cake tin.

To make the pastry, use electric beaters to beat the
butter and sugar together until creamy and pale, about
1 minute. Beat in the egg and vanilla. Mix in the flour and
baking powder. Switching to mix with your hands, knead
quickly to incorporate everything. Put aside one-third
of the dough (about 150 g/5½ oz) to make the biscuits.
Press the two-thirds of dough firmly onto the bottom and
two-thirds of the way up the side of the prepared tin.

For the filling, prepare the fruit — halve strawberries
and cherries if large, remove stones and slice stone fruit,
and cut other large fruit into big chunky slices. Put in a
bowl and sprinkle with the 2 tablespoons raw sugar. Turn
through gently. Distribute the fruit evenly over the crust.
Bake for about 50 minutes or until the fruit looks lovely
and jammy, trapped in a cage of pastry. Remove from
the oven to cool. Dust with icing sugar and serve in slices,
alone or with whipped cream.

BISCUITS

Bake these while you finish the tart. Break off 10 pieces of
the reserved dough, each about the size of a walnut, and
roll in your palms. Flatten slightly. Place on a baking tray
lined with baking paper, leaving space for spreading. With
the dough that's left, make decorations such as initials
and put on top of the biscuits. Bake for 10 minutes or so,
until golden. Offer as treats or snacks.

FILOMENA'S APPLE CAKE

150 g (5½ oz) BUTTER, SOFTENED

150 g (5½ oz) SUGAR, PLUS
2 TABLESPOONS, EXTRA

2 TEASPOONS VANILLA EXTRACT

3 EGGS, SEPARATED

250 g (9 oz/1⅔ cups) PLAIN
(ALL-PURPOSE) FLOUR

2 TABLESPOONS POTATO FLOUR

2 TEASPOONS BAKING POWDER

3 TABLESPOONS MILK

3 RENNET APPLES
(OR OTHER LARGE SWEET
COOKING APPLES), ABOUT
220 g (7¾ oz) EACH

ICING (CONFECTIONERS')
SUGAR, FOR DUSTING

*Makes a 24 cm
(9½ inch) cake*

This is somewhere between a cake and a tart. It is my friend Marta's mother's recipe. When I made it and took it to Marta you could see she was nicely surprised by my effort. It's quite fun when you make someone's own recipe and take it to them! Anyway, Marta was adamant that next time I use rennet apples as I had used whatever I could get that day. She said 'No, no, no. Tttt, ttt, ttt. Rennet.'

Preheat the oven to 170°C (325°F/Gas 3). Butter and flour a round 24 cm (9½ inch) springform cake tin.

Using electric beaters, whip the butter and sugar in a wide bowl until creamy. Add the vanilla, then add the egg yolks 1 at a time, whisking well after each. Whisk in the flour, potato flour and baking powder, adding the milk as the mixture thickens to make it come together in a very thick batter. Scrape the mixture off the beaters into the bowl, then wash and dry them. Use the clean beaters to whip the egg whites to snowy peaks. Using a metal spoon, fold a scoop of the egg whites into the cake batter until evenly dispersed, then gently fold in the rest of the whites. If they are difficult to incorporate, give a quick whisk with the electric beaters to mix it all together. Scrape into the prepared tin and level the surface.

Peel, core and halve the apples. Cut across the halves into slices of 4–5 mm (⅛–¼ inch). Starting at the centre of the cake, arrange the slices slightly obliquely, pushed about halfway into the batter. Pack them tightly together, working your way outwards like the petals of a rose. It may seem like there is too much apple, but fill in any spaces as it will look lovely later. Scatter the extra 2 tablespoons of sugar evenly over the top. Bake until the apples begin to get golden and some of the edges are dark, about 45 minutes, then cover with foil and continue baking for a further 15–20 minutes or until the cake is ready. (The middle should look ever-so-faintly gooey.) It is important that the cake is not overcooked as the edges and bottom will dry out. Remove the foil and cool before removing from the tin. Serve dusted lightly with icing sugar.

RADICCHIO CAKE WITH WHITE CHOCOLATE ICING

ABOUT 1 TABLESPOON
DRY BREADCRUMBS

ABOUT 1 litre (35 fl oz/
4 cups) WATER

2 TABLESPOONS SUGAR,
PLUS 100 g (3½ oz),
EXTRA

150 g (5½ oz) TRIMMED
ROUND RADICCHIO
(½ A SMALL ONE)

100 g (3½ oz)
BUTTER, SOFTENED

3 EGGS

1 TEASPOON FINELY
GRATED LEMON RIND,
YELLOW PART ONLY

1 TABLESPOON BRANDY

1 TEASPOON
VANILLA EXTRACT

A GOOD GRATING
OF NUTMEG

125 g (4½ oz) PLAIN
(ALL-PURPOSE) FLOUR

2 TEASPOONS
BAKING POWDER

WHITE CHOCOLATE ICING

150 g (5½ oz) WHITE
CHOCOLATE, CHOPPED

Makes a 20 cm (8 inch) cake

This is my sister-in-law Luisa's recipe. It comes from Chioggia, where they have lots of radicchio. It is surprisingly good with a lovely texture, and it keeps well.

Preheat the oven to 180°C (350°F/Gas 4). Butter a round 20 cm (8 inch) springform cake tin. Scatter the breadcrumbs in and shake it so the breadcrumbs stick to the butter. Shake out the excess.

Bring the water to the boil with the 2 tablespoons of sugar. Loosen the radicchio leaves and add to the boiling water. Cook for a few minutes to soften. Drain and pat dry with paper towels, then chop up.

Using electric beaters, whip the butter with the extra sugar until creamy. Whip the eggs in one by one, then add the lemon rind, brandy, vanilla and nutmeg, whisking in to blend. Add the flour, baking powder and a pinch of salt, whisking until smooth. Fold in the cooled radicchio. Scrape the mixture into the prepared tin and bake for about 40 minutes or until a skewer inserted in the centre comes out clean. Remove from the oven and cool completely before removing from the tin.

For the icing, melt the chocolate in a bain marie (see Glossary). When it has cooled a little and begun to thicken spread it thickly over the top of the cake.

TORTA TARTUFATA

◇◇◇

THE
LIST

40 g (1½ oz) HAZELNUTS, SKINNED

100 g (3½ oz) BUTTER

120 g (4¼ oz) DARK UNSWEETENED CHOCOLATE, CHOPPED

2 TABLESPOONS UNSWEETENED COCOA POWDER

3 EGGS, SEPARATED

100 g (3½ oz) SUGAR

½ TEASPOON VANILLA EXTRACT

20 g (¾ oz) PLAIN (ALL-PURPOSE) FLOUR

ICING (CONFECTIONERS') SUGAR, FOR DUSTING

———

Makes a 28 cm (11¼ inch) cake

This is Marzia's recipe. She adores baking and is always honoured to give out her recipes. This is a nice, flat chocolate cake. Easy to make, easy to eat. Its name is truffle cake because it is chocolatey and moist.

Preheat the oven to 180°C (350°F/Gas 4). Butter and flour a round 28 cm (11¼ inch) springform cake tin. Toast the hazelnuts in a dry frying pan just enough to draw out their flavour. Coarsely chop the nuts, leaving good texture.

Melt the butter in a saucepan and add the chocolate and cocoa. Stir until the chocolate has melted and is smooth, then remove from the heat. Leave to cool. Using electric beaters, whip the egg whites in a bowl to snowy peaks, then keep aside for now. Use the electric beaters to whip the egg yolks, sugar and vanilla in a generous wide bowl until creamy. Stir in the chocolate mixture. Next, whisk in the flour, nuts and a pinch of salt. Finally, gently fold in the creamy egg whites with a metal spoon, folding from the bottom to the top as though you are drawing circles with the spoon in the batter.

Scrape out into the prepared tin and bake for about 20 minutes or until the top looks like dry desert soil, but the middle is still humid and soft. Cool before serving with a light dusting of icing sugar.

CHOCOLATE SPREAD

THE
LIST

70 g (2½ oz) BUTTER

4 TABLESPOONS MILK

120 g (4¼ oz) DARK UNSWEETENED CHOCOLATE, CHOPPED

60 g (2¼ oz) SUGAR

———

Makes just under 1 cup

This is a simple chocolate spread you can put on bread. It's also great on a just-cooked plain pizza base, scattered with toasted hazelnuts (see Sweet pizza, page 61).

Set up a bain marie (see Glossary). Put the butter, milk and chocolate in the bowl. When it starts melting add the sugar, stirring until it is thick and smooth. Cool. It will keep in a closed jar in a cool place for about 10 days.

LEMON VERBENA PEACHES & CREAM

THE LIST

50 g (1¾ oz) SUGAR

500 ml (17 fl oz/2 cups) WATER

1 TABLESPOON HONEY

4 WHITE PEACHES (WITH RED STREAKS), ABOUT 600 g (1 lb 5 oz) IN TOTAL

5 GENEROUS SPRIGS (10 cm/4 inches OR SO EACH) FRESH LEMON VERBENA, PLUS EXTRA, TO SERVE, IF YOU LIKE

MASCARPONE CREAM

185 ml (6 fl oz/¾ cup) POURING (WHIPPING) CREAM

150 g (5½ oz) MASCARPONE

2 TEASPOONS ICING (CONFECTIONERS') SUGAR

A FEW DROPS OF VANILLA EXTRACT

Serves 4

This is beautiful and refreshing. It's worth growing lemon verbena in your garden for its incredible smell alone. Before it dries up for the winter I collect and dry as many leaves as I can and then I can't wait for summer again. I always drink it as a tea with a little honey.

Here, I have poached peaches in a lemon verbena infusion. The peaches I love are white with tinges of red in their skin and through their flesh. This gives a beautiful colour to the syrup. If you can't get these peaches, add a couple of raspberries to the poaching liquid.

Put the sugar, water and honey in a pot just big enough to take the peaches side by side. Bring to the boil, then reduce the heat to a simmer and add the whole peaches. If necessary, top up the water level to just cover the peaches (but not so much that the syrup will be diluted). Tuck in the lemon verbena. Tear off a square of baking paper larger than the diameter of your pot and press it down onto the tops of the peaches. Simmer gently (rapid boiling may cause the fruit to break up) until poached, but still firm and holding their shape well, about 8 minutes.

Remove the peaches to a flat bowl to cool for a bit. When they're cool enough to handle, slip off the skins — they should come away like silk dresses. If not, return them to their bath to simmer a while longer. Leave the syrup in the pot to cool.

Meanwhile, make the mascarpone cream. In a small bowl, gradually mix together the cream and mascarpone. Add the icing sugar and vanilla, and beat until smooth.

Serve a cooled peach in a flat bowl with syrup and a good spoonful of mascarpone cream.

SAPIENTE
WORDS/PAROLE

IF SOMETHING IS WORTH DOING,
IT'S WORTH DOING WELL

ROSE BISCUITS

75 g (2¾ oz)
BUTTER, SOFTENED

75 g (2¾ oz) SUGAR,
PLUS A LITTLE EXTRA,
FOR SPRINKLING

1 EGG

A FEW DROPS OF
VANILLA EXTRACT

1 TEASPOON ROSEWATER

210 g (7½ oz) PLAIN
(ALL-PURPOSE) FLOUR

TINY FRESH UNSPRAYED
ROSEBUDS OR ONES YOU
HAVE DRIED (SEE PAGE 282),
HALVED LENGTHWAYS

ABOUT 1 TEASPOON
GUM ARABIC, IF USING
DRIED ROSEBUDS

Makes 15

These are true beauties. You can set fresh rosebuds on them before baking or stick dried ones on top after baking. You can also fold dried rose petals into some of the dough before shaping the biscuits for a variation (these wouldn't need a rosebud on top). The rosebuds are edible, but you might prefer to pick them off before eating.

Preheat the oven to 170°C (325°F/Gas 3) and line a baking tray with baking paper. Using electric beaters, cream the butter and sugar together until pale and thick. Beat in the egg, then add the vanilla and rosewater. Add the flour and mix in with a wooden spoon. You can keep the dough in the fridge or make the biscuits immediately.

Break off balls of dough the size of a rum ball, just under 20 g (¾ oz) each. I like them best at 18 g, to be exact. Roll them into smooth balls with your hands. Flatten them ever so slightly, then place on the lined tray, leaving a little space between each. Use a plastic bottle cap (from a bottle of water, for example) to gently press a ring pattern on the top of each biscuit. If using fresh rosebuds, set a half on top of each biscuit, pressing it in gently. Sprinkle a little extra sugar over the top. Bake for 10 minutes, until just set but still very pale (they will harden as they cool). Move them to a wire rack to cool.

If using dried rosebuds, you can put them on now. Mix a little gum arabic with enough water to give a sticky paste. Using a toothpick, put a few drops on the cut side of a rosebud and press it gently onto the biscuit.

DRYING ROSEBUDS
& VIOLETS

◇◇

Gather tiny unsprayed rosebuds and violets that have
no dew or water on them. Spread on a tray and put in a
dry sunny spot indoors; for example, in front of a window.
Leave until completely dried, turning them over now and
then, and opening out any petals that may have curled in.
Violets will be ready in a matter of days, but rosebuds will
need longer.

LEMON BISCUITS
WITH VIOLETS

◇◇

THE
––––––––– LIST –––––––––

75 g (2¾ oz)
BUTTER, SOFTENED

75 g (2¾ oz) SUGAR,
PLUS A LITTLE EXTRA,
FOR SPRINKLING

1 EGG

A FEW DROPS OF
VANILLA EXTRACT

½ TEASPOON GRATED
LEMON RIND, YELLOW
PART ONLY

210 g (7½ oz) PLAIN
(ALL-PURPOSE) FLOUR

ABOUT 1 TEASPOON
GUM ARABIC

ABOUT 20 DRIED
UNSPRAYED VIOLETS

––––––

Makes 20

Preheat the oven to 170°C (325°F/Gas 3) and line a baking
tray with baking paper. Using electric beaters, cream the
butter and sugar together until pale and thick. Beat in the
egg, then add the vanilla and lemon rind. Add the flour
and mix in with a wooden spoon. You can keep the dough
in the fridge or make the biscuits immediately.

Break off balls of dough the size of a rum ball, just
under 20 g (¾ oz) each. I like them best at 18 g, to be
exact. Roll them into smooth balls with your hands. Flatten
them ever so slightly, then place on the lined tray, leaving
a little space between each. Sprinkle a good pinch of
sugar over the tops. Use a plastic bottle cap (from a bottle
of water, for example) to gently press a ring pattern on top
of each biscuit. This gives them a nice shape when baked.
Bake for 10 minutes, until just set but still very pale (they
will harden as they cool). Move them to a wire rack to cool.

Mix a little gum arabic with enough water to give a
sticky paste. Using a toothpick, put a few drops on the
underside of a violet and press gently onto a biscuit.

SAPIENTE

WORDS/PAROLE

A PLACE FOR EVERYTHING AND
EVERYTHING IN ITS PLACE

LAVENDER BISCUITS

THE
LIST

75 g (2¾ oz)
BUTTER, SOFTENED

75 g (2¾ oz) LAVENDER
SUGAR (PAGE 42)

1 EGG

A FEW DROPS OF
VANILLA EXTRACT

210 g (7 ½ oz) PLAIN
(ALL-PURPOSE) FLOUR

ABOUT 20 FRESH UNSPRAYED
LAVENDER FLOWER TIPS

SUGAR, FOR
SPRINKLING

Makes 20

Preheat the oven to 170°C (325°F/Gas 3) and line a baking tray with baking paper. Put the butter and lavender sugar in a bowl and use electric beaters to beat well, until a little pale and the sugar has dissolved, about 30 seconds. Beat in the egg and vanilla. Add the flour and mix through with a wooden spoon. Keep the dough in the fridge or make the biscuits immediately.

Break off balls of dough the size of a rum ball, about 20 g (¾ oz) each. Roll them into smooth balls with your hands, then flatten them a bit. Place on the lined tray and press a lavender tip gently onto the top of each. Sprinkle with a little sugar and bake for about 10 minutes, until just set but still very pale (they will harden as they cool). Move them to a wire rack to cool.

CROSTATA DI CREMA

CREMA

2 EGG YOLKS

60 g (2¼ oz) SUGAR

½ TEASPOON
VANILLA EXTRACT

30 g (1 oz) PLAIN
(ALL-PURPOSE) FLOUR

200 ml (7 fl oz) MILK

200 ml (7 fl oz) POURING
(WHIPPING) CREAM

3–4 cm (1¼–1½ inch)
STRIP LEMON RIND,
YELLOW PART ONLY

PASTRY

250 g (9 oz/1²/₃ cups) PLAIN
(ALL-PURPOSE) FLOUR

65 g (2¼ oz) BUTTER,
CUT UP INTO CUBES

1 EGG YOLK

1 WHOLE EGG

80 g (2¾ oz) SUGAR

ICING (CONFECTIONERS')
SUGAR, FOR DUSTING

*Makes a 24 cm
(9½ inch) tart*

I like this plain, sometimes with a raspberry put in each window while it is still warm. You can brush a little of the unused egg whites over the pastry before baking, then put the rest towards Nonna's egg white cake (page 289).

To make the crema, in a heavy-bottomed pot whip the egg yolks, sugar and vanilla until thick and creamy. Whip in the flour until smooth. Add a little of the milk to amalgamate, then whip in the rest of the milk and the cream. Add the lemon rind. Put over low heat and bring to a very gentle boil, whisking all the time until it thickens. Remove from the heat and let it cool, whisking every now and then to prevent lumps forming.

Preheat the oven to 170°C (325°F/Gas 3). Butter a round 24 cm (9½ inch) springform cake tin.

To make the pastry, put the flour and a pinch of salt in a bowl. Rub the butter in well with your fingertips. Add the egg yolk, whole egg and sugar and knead lightly until it all comes together. Roll out two-thirds of the pastry into a disc, roughly 30 cm (12 inches) in diameter. Ease the pastry into the tin, to cover the bottom and come about halfway up the side. Divide the remaining third of pastry into 12 portions and roll these on a lightly floured surface into thin ropes of varying lengths.

Plop the cooled crema into the middle of the pastry case and spread out lightly with a spatula. Lay the pastry ropes over, half going one way and half cross-hatching the other way. Trim the ends and neaten the sides. Brush the pastry lightly with egg white, using a narrow brush. Bake for 35–40 minutes or until the pastry is golden and crisp. Cool, then dust with icing sugar and serve in slices.

CROSTATA
WITH PEACH JAM

100 g (3½ oz) BUTTER, SOFTENED

350 g (12 oz/2⅓ cups) PLAIN (ALL-PURPOSE) FLOUR

180 g (6¼ oz) SUGAR

2 EGGS, LIGHTLY BEATEN

½ TEASPOON BAKING POWDER

400 g (14 oz) PEACH JAM (PAGE 39) OR OTHER JAM

1 EGG YOLK, WHISKED, FOR GLAZING

Makes a 28 cm (11¼ inch) tart

This is delicious and quick to make. Use your favourite jam – it looks super with a red jam, too. I like to make two of these with different colour jams and serve a slice of each. You can use a little milk to brush over the pastry if you don't want to use up an egg yolk, but the yolk will give you a glossier and deeper colour.

Put the butter in a bowl with the flour, sugar, eggs, baking powder and a pinch of salt and mix together well. Knead the dough into a compact ball, flatten a bit and wrap in plastic wrap. Chill in the fridge for half an hour or so.

Preheat the oven to 180°C (350°F/Gas 4). Butter a round 28 cm (11¼ inch) loose-based tart tin.

Break off one-third or so of the pastry and keep to one side. On a large sheet of baking paper, roll out the larger piece of dough into a circle of about 34 cm (13½ inches), as it needs to go up and above the side of the tin. Using the baking paper as a tray, position it over the tin and then flip it so the pastry is underneath. Quickly ease it into the tin and peel away the baking paper. Work the pastry over the base and up the side of the tin, pressing it gently into place. Prick the bottom here and there with a fork. Spoon the jam in and spread it to cover the pastry evenly. Turn the sides of the pastry down over the jam to neaten.

Roll the remaining one-third of dough into 18 ropes of various lengths to cover the tart in a criss-cross diamond pattern. Lay them in place, then trim the ends. Using a small brush, brush the pastry with the whisked egg yolk. Bake for 25–30 minutes or until the pastry is deep golden and the bottom crisp. Cool before slicing. This keeps well, covered, for a few days.

NONNA'S EGG WHITE CAKE

This is what Nonna does to use up egg whites after using the yolks in a cream or elsewhere. It is lovely as a cake, but quite special turned into Cantuccini (see below).

Preheat the oven to 170°C (325°F/Gas 3). Butter a round 24 cm (9½ inch) springform cake tin and line the base with baking paper.

Using electric beaters, first whisk the egg whites in a bowl until white and snowy. Keep aside. Without washing the beaters whisk the sugar, butter and vanilla in a separate bowl until the sugar has dissolved. Use a wooden spoon to mix in the lemon rind and then the flour, baking powder, ground almonds, potato flour and a pinch of salt. The mixture will be very stiff.

Using a metal spoon, fold one-third of the egg whites into the mixture until evenly dispersed, then gently fold in the rest of the whites. If they are difficult to incorporate give a quick whisk with the electric beaters to mix it all in. Spoon the mixture into the prepared tin and bake for 25–30 minutes or until springy and a skewer inserted in the middle comes out clean. Cool.

CANTUCCINI

Preheat the oven to 120°C (235°F/Gas ½) and line a baking tray with baking paper. Slice right across the cake to make strips 1.5 cm (⅝ inch) thick. Cut these into 2 or 3 long lengths and lay on their sides on the lined tray. Bake until dry and golden, about 40 minutes. Remove from the oven and cool on the tray. Store in a biscuit tin where they will keep for many weeks.

THE LIST

4 EGG WHITES

150 g (5½ oz) SUGAR

100 g (3½ oz) BUTTER, MELTED

1 TEASPOON VANILLA EXTRACT

1 TEASPOON FINELY GRATED LEMON RIND, YELLOW PART ONLY

100 g (3½ oz/⅔ cup) PLAIN (ALL-PURPOSE) FLOUR

1 TEASPOON BAKING POWDER

50 g (1¾ oz/½ cup) GROUND ALMONDS

50 g (1¾ oz) POTATO FLOUR

Makes a 24 cm (9½ inch) cake

TORTA CAMPAGNOLA

2 EGGS, SEPARATED

150 g (5½ oz) SUGAR

GRATED RIND OF 1 LEMON,
YELLOW PART ONLY

JUICE OF 1 LEMON

1 TEASPOON VANILLA
EXTRACT

6 TABLESPOONS OLIVE OIL

180 ml (6 fl oz) MILK

300 g (10½ oz/2 cups) PLAIN
(ALL-PURPOSE) FLOUR

4 TEASPOONS
BAKING POWDER

*Makes a 24 cm
(9½ inch) cake*

*Simple, feathery light and wonderful for breakfast.
Or anytime really. The kind of cake your grandmother
will have made.*

Preheat the oven to 180°C (350°F/Gas 4). Butter and flour
a round 24 cm (9½ inch) springform cake tin.

Whip the egg whites to snowy peaks in a bowl first so
you don't have to wash the beaters. In another bowl, use
the beaters to whip the egg yolks, sugar, lemon rind and
juice, vanilla and olive oil until creamy. Add the milk and
mix in well to blend. Beat in the flour and baking powder.

Fold the beaten egg whites through and scrape out
into the prepared tin. Bake for about 30–35 minutes, until
beautiful, golden and risen, and a skewer inserted in the
middle comes out clean. It will probably have a nice crack
across the top.

TORTA MIMOSA

CAKE

6 EGGS, SEPARATED

180 g (6¼ oz) SUGAR

½ TEASPOON
VANILLA EXTRACT

100 g (3½ oz/⅔ cup)
PLAIN (ALL-PURPOSE) FLOUR

50 g (1¾ oz) POTATO FLOUR

4 TEASPOONS
BAKING POWDER

*Makes a 24 cm
(9½ inch) cake*

*The mimosa flower is a symbol of the strength and
love of women. In Italy, on the 'Festa della Donna' on
the 8th of March it is common to give a few sprigs of
the bright yellow blossoms to female friends, colleagues
or anyone special to you. Torta mimosa is abundant at
this time of year. Use eggs with very yellow yolks for the
best colour. The cake can be made a day ahead and
assembled on the day of serving.*

Preheat the oven to 180°C (350°F/Gas 4). Butter
and flour a round 24 cm (9½ inch) springform cake tin.

To make the cake, use electric beaters to whip the egg
whites to snowy peaks. In a separate bowl, whip the egg
yolks, sugar and vanilla. Combine the flour, potato flour
and baking powder and whisk into the yolk mixture. Fold a
scoop of egg whites through and when that is combined,
fold in the rest. Scoop the mixture into the prepared tin,

CREMA

480 ml (16½ fl oz) MILK

A FEW DROPS OF
VANILLA EXTRACT

SMALL STRIP OF LEMON
RIND, YELLOW PART ONLY

4 EGG YOLKS

100 g (3½ oz) SUGAR

25 g (1 oz) PLAIN
(ALL-PURPOSE) FLOUR

125 ml (4 fl oz/½ cup)
POURING (WHIPPING) CREAM

2 TABLESPOONS
BOUGHT OR HOME-MADE
LIMONCELLO (PAGE 17)

level the surface and bake for about 30 minutes or until golden and a skewer inserted in the centre comes out clean. Cool in the tin for 10 minutes, then turn out onto a wire rack and cool completely.

To make the crema, heat the milk, vanilla and lemon rind in a medium saucepan to just below boiling. Use electric beaters to cream the egg yolks and sugar in a bowl. When they are pale and thick, mix in the flour. Whisk a little of the near-boiling milk into the egg mixture and then add the rest, whisking all the time. Now pour it all back into the saucepan and cook over low heat, stirring, until the mixture is thick and smooth. Take off the heat and cool completely, stirring often as it cools.

Whip the cream to stiff peaks. Remove the lemon rind from the crema and fold the whipped cream through.

Slice the cake in half horizontally. Carefully pluck out the centre of the cut side of each half, 5 mm to 1 cm (¼–½ inch) deep and leaving a border of about 1 cm (½ inch). Reserve the part you've taken out. Splash the limoncello evenly over the cut sides. Put the bottom half of the cake on a large flat plate, cut side up. Spoon two-thirds of the crema into the centre and spread evenly, then position the top half of the cake in place. Spread the rest of the crema over the top and sides of the cake.

Use your fingers to crumble the reserved cake into fairly uniform bits that look like mimosa blossoms. Scatter them over the top and sides of the cake, pressing them gently onto the crema to stick. Cover the cake as evenly as you can. The cake is now ready to serve. It will keep well in a cake tin in a cool spot for a couple of days.

SAPIENTE
WORDS/PAROLE

THE CHILDREN OF MY CHILDREN
ARE TWICE MY CHILDREN

GRANNY JOY'S MARMALADE CAKE

Use home-made (page 38) or bought orange marmalade
here. You can have this lovely cake for afternoon tea
or you might like to serve it after a meal with a little
whipped cream on the side.

Preheat the oven to 180°C (350°F/Gas 4). Butter and flour
a round 24 cm (9½ inch) springform cake tin or, if you
prefer, a bundt tin.

Using electric beaters, cream the butter and sugar
together in a mixing bowl. Add the eggs one by one,
beating well after each. Add the vanilla, marmalade and
orange rind. Beat in the flour and baking powder.

Scrape out into the prepared tin and bake for about
40 minutes, until golden and set. Test with a knitting
needle — stick it in the centre of the cake and if it comes
out clean the cake is done. Cool before turning out and
dribbling with the glaze.

To make the glaze, stir the orange juice into the icing
sugar until dissolved and smooth.

THE LIST

180 g (6¼ oz) BUTTER,
SOFTENED

180 g (6¼ oz) SUGAR

3 EGGS

1 TEASPOON VANILLA
EXTRACT

6 TABLESPOONS ORANGE
MARMALADE

1 TABLESPOON GRATED
ORANGE RIND, ORANGE
PART ONLY

180 g (6¼ oz) PLAIN
(ALL-PURPOSE) FLOUR

1½ TEASPOONS
BAKING POWDER

GLAZE

2 TABLESPOONS ORANGE JUICE

60 g (2¼ oz/½ cup) ICING
(CONFECTIONERS') SUGAR

*Makes a 24 cm
(9½ inch) cake*

NONNA'S
DOLCE DI MARIE

160 g (5½ oz) SUGAR

120 ml (4 fl oz) STRONG
ESPRESSO COFFEE, COOLED

200 g (7 oz) BUTTER, SOFTENED

300 g (10½ oz) RECTANGULAR
MARIE (PETIT BEURRE) BISCUITS

30 g (1 oz) DARK UNSWEETENED
CHOCOLATE, GRATED

ABOUT 1 TEASPOON
GROUND COFFEE BEANS

Serves quite a few

*I was surprised when various friends told me of this
cake that their nonnas made. And when I made it I was
surprised to find everyone still likes it, even if they haven't
had it for years. It would have been the kind of thing that
was thrown together with simple ingredients always on
hand. It reminds me of the Marie biscuits we used to have
as children — one with a layer of butter, another with
a layer of jam and sandwiched together.*

Add 1 tablespoon of the sugar to the espresso coffee
and stir until it dissolves. Pour into a flat bowl. Using
electric beaters, cream the remaining sugar and the
butter together until smooth and pale.

You will need a rectangular dish close to 25 x 18 cm
(10 x 7 inches). Start with a single layer of biscuits. Dip
the biscuits one by one in the coffee, making sure they
are bathed on both sides but not so much that they go
soggy or fall apart. Lay them on the bottom of the dish
to completely cover it. Spatula one-quarter of the butter
cream over, spreading it evenly. Next, scatter one-quarter
of the chocolate over the top. Take a pinch of the ground
coffee and scatter that over the chocolate.

Repeat the procession three more times, finishing with
a final scattering of chocolate and ground coffee. Your
work is done. Put it in the fridge for an hour or two before
cutting off a small square for a snack. It's rather rich,
so you judge how big you want the squares to be.

SAPIENTE
WORDS/PAROLE

IF LIFE GIVES YOU LEMONS,
MAKE LEMON PIE

125 g (4½ oz)
BUTTER, CHOPPED

125 g (4½ oz) RECTANGULAR
MARIE (PETIT BEURRE)
OR DIGESTIVE BISCUITS

250 ml (9 fl oz/1 cup)
POURING (WHIPPING) CREAM

340 g (11¾ oz)
CONDENSED MILK

JUICE OF 2 LARGE LEMONS

Serves a family

LEMON PIE

This is my sister Ludi's recipe. She can make it with her eyes closed. It has a nice, old-fashioned atmosphere to it. I get the feeling the original recipe must have come from the back of a condensed milk tin years ago. Whatever the case may be, it's lemon heaven. It is as easy as it can get to make a pie, though it needs a good few hours to set and hold in the fridge, so making it the day before is perfect. You can scatter a handful of chopped almonds over the top if you like, or just serve it plain.

Put the butter in a 22 x 16 cm (8½ x 6¼ inch) flameproof ceramic or glass dish and put it in the sun, on top of the heater or on the stovetop to melt. Crush the biscuits in a food processor or blender. Add to the butter and mix well. Press firmly and evenly onto the base of the dish.
  Whip the cream until fairly stiff. Add the condensed milk and whip to incorporate. Now for the magic – quickly whisk in the lemon juice and see how the mixture thickens! Scrape out over the biscuit base and level the surface. Cover the dish with plastic wrap and refrigerate until set. When ready to serve, take the dish from the fridge and cut into not very big, loose squares. If the base seems too firm to cut, leave it at room temperature for 10 minutes or so and then cut.

180 g (6¼ oz) BLANCHED
ALMONDS

180 g (6¼ oz) SUGAR

180 g (6¼ oz) BUTTER,
AT ROOM TEMPERATURE

200 g (7 oz/1⅓ cups) PLAIN
(ALL-PURPOSE) FLOUR

ABOUT 100 g (3½ oz) DARK
UNSWEETENED
CHOCOLATE

Makes about 35

BACI DI DAMA

*Also known as Lady's or Dame's kisses, many places in
Italy have these wonderfully crisp biscuits, sandwiched
together with a layer of dark chocolate. What could
possibly be wrong with that?*

Toast the nuts lightly in a dry frying pan, taking care not to
burn them. Cool a bit, then grind with a tablespoon or so
of the sugar. Cream the remaining sugar and butter using
electric beaters. Add the flour and then the nuts, mixing
by hand now to incorporate. Put in the fridge for a while
so the dough is easier to work with.

Preheat the oven to 170°C (325°F/Gas 3). Line 2 baking
trays with baking paper.

Break off balls of dough the size of a cherry, about
10 g (¼ oz) each. Put them on the prepared trays, leaving
a little space between each for spreading. Bake for about
20 minutes, until pale gold. Remove and cool.

Meanwhile, melt the chocolate in a bain marie
(see Glossary). Stir until smooth, then remove from the
heat and cool a little but don't let it set again. Using a
teaspoon, dab some melted chocolate (not so much that
it oozes out) on the bottom of a biscuit and grab a partner
for it. Gently press the two together. Continue until all the
couples are taken. Put them on a wire rack to set and stay
together, and then you can move them to a pretty lined
tray or a lovely tin.

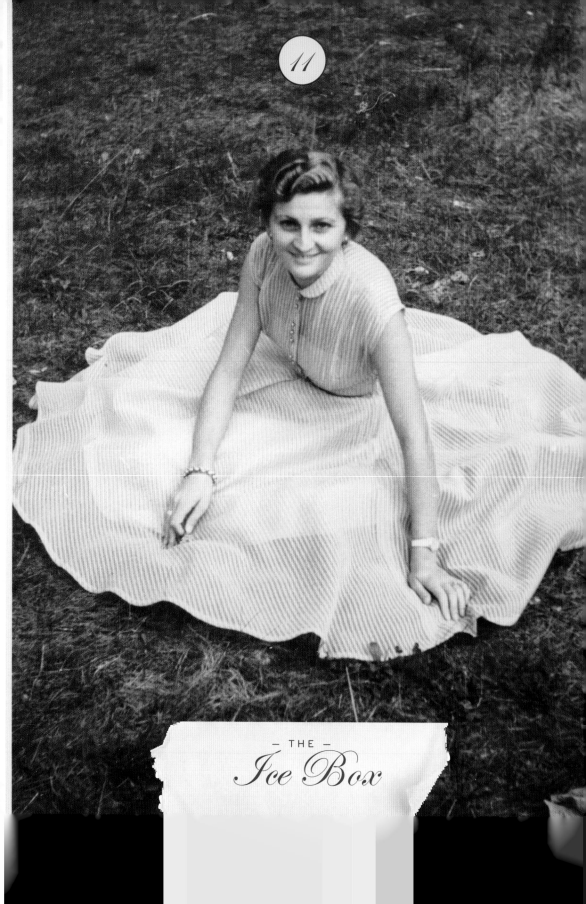

— THE —

Ice Box

BACI DI SIENA

MASCARPONE & LAVENDER ICE CREAM
WITH WILD STRAWBERRIES

GRANITA DI MANDORLE

PAN BRIOCHE

COFFEE & CASSIA ICE CREAM

GIANDUIA ICE CREAM MATTONE
WITH WHIPPED CREAM

MILK & MINT ICE CREAM

LIMONCELLO SORBET

FIOR DI LATTE ICE CREAM

One

THERE SEEMS TO
BE A SECRET CODE
AMONG WOMEN. AN
UNSPOKEN GUARANTEE
THAT WILL BREAK
SILENCES. HOLD
THINGS UP. LET YOU
STEP OVER BARRIERS.
CROSS BOUNDARIES
TO COLLECT THINGS.
RECIPES. A RECIPE
IS THE SECRET CODE
THAT ALLOWS YOU
TO SHARE SPACE AND
TIME WITH ANOTHER IN
THE LINE AT THE

THE ICE BOX

BUTCHER, BAKER OR
CANDLESTICK MAKER.
LIKE A GIFT TO BE
PASSED ON.

+ *Truth* +

+ **LOVE** +

& *Honour* &

No. 118.

Two

MANY WOMEN
CONSIDER IT PRECIOUS
KNOWLEDGE THAT
MUST BE PASSED ON
FROM WOMAN TO
WOMAN AND BE SAVED.
THEIR MISSION IS TO
PRACTISE THE ART AND
PASS IT ON. THIS CODE
SEEMS TO UNITE MOST
WOMEN. AND FOR
A WOMAN A RECIPE IS
LIKE A TROPHY. THIS
IS HER WAY. HER BEST
SALSA. HER BEST CAKE

THE ICE BOX

THAT DESERVES AN
AWARD. WHEN WE HEAR
OF AN OLDER WOMAN
WHO IS A GREAT COOK
SHE COMMANDS
RESPECT. SHE IS
A SUPERWOMAN.
A TROPHY TAKER.

No. 118.

SAPIENTE

WORDS/PAROLE

TO A VALIANT HEART,
NOTHING IS IMPOSSIBLE

THE
LIST

**250 ml (9 fl oz/1 cup)
POURING (WHIPPING) CREAM**

**400 g (14 oz) DARK
UNSWEETENED CHOCOLATE**

**100 g (3½ oz) HARD NOUGAT,
COARSELY CHOPPED**

**1½ TABLESPOONS
OLIVE OIL**

Makes about 10

BACI DI SIENA

I love finding this kind of thing in the freezer, and evidently so does everyone else, because whenever I make them and go back to get more there are none. Each will make one rich portion or they can be shared.

Whip the cream stiffly, as it has to hold all the other ingredients. Chop 20 g (¾ oz) or so of the chocolate into bits. Add to the cream, along with the nougat and fold through. Line a tray that will fit in your freezer with baking paper. Scoop up 1 tablespoon of the cream and use another tablespoon to edge it off onto the baking paper to form a small hill. When all the cream has been used put the tray in the freezer for about an hour to set the hills.

Melt the remaining chocolate in a bain marie (see Glossary), stirring with a wooden spoon. Remove from the heat, stir in the olive oil and cool a little. It needs to be liquid, but not hot, for dipping. When the hills are frozen drop them one at a time into the chocolate and turn them over using 2 tablespoons to coat completely on all sides. Set them back on the tray and return to the freezer to set the chocolate. Once set, wrap them up in foil and tie with a ribbon. Keep in the freezer and serve directly from there.

MASCARPONE &
LAVENDER ICE CREAM
WITH WILD STRAWBERRIES

THE
LIST

250 ml (9 fl oz/1 cup) MILK

1 HEAPED TEASPOON
UNSPRAYED LAVENDER FLOWERS

3 EGG YOLKS

100 g (3½ oz) SUGAR

1 TEASPOON VANILLA EXTRACT

250 g (9 oz) MASCARPONE

A SMALL CUPPED HANDFUL
OF WILD STRAWBERRIES
PER PERSON, TO SERVE

Serves 6–8

This ice cream freshens you up, leaving a gentle hint of lavender lingering on. You can use fresh or dried lavender. Fresh lavender flowers should be collected in branches at the end of summer, then left to dry in bunches. I love this with wild strawberries when they are in season. You can keep the egg whites towards another use such as Nonna's egg white cake (page 289) or they can be stored in the freezer, with a label to remind you how many there are.

Put the milk in a medium pot and bring slowly to the boil. Add the lavender flowers just before it gets there and then take the pot off the heat. Leave for about 10 minutes to infuse, stirring so the lavender perfumes the milk.

Use electric beaters to beat the egg yolks, sugar and vanilla in a medium bowl until pale, thick and creamy. Strain the perfumed milk into the egg mixture, whisking to incorporate so the eggs don't curdle. Return all the mixture to the pan and cook over low heat until slightly thickened. It is important to use a very low heat and whisk for just a short time so the eggs don't curdle. Set aside to cool for 5 to 10 minutes, stirring every now and then.

Whisk in the mascarpone until free of lumps, then cool completely. Churn in an ice-cream machine following the manufacturer's instructions. Alternatively, pour into a shallow tray and put in the freezer. When it is just frozen, after about 1 hour, beat vigorously with a fork to break up the ice crystals and then return the tray to the freezer. Repeat this process twice before leaving it to freeze completely. Keep in the freezer in a sealed container.

If the ice cream seems too hard to serve initially, leave it at room temperature to soften slightly. Serve scoops of the ice cream with some wild strawberries.

Rose

Il profumo dei fiori

GRANITA DI MANDORLE

250 g (9 oz) BLANCHED
ALMONDS

130 g (4½ oz) SUGAR

700 ml (24 fl oz) WATER

Makes 2½–3 cups

This is adored in Sicily, especially as breakfast in summer. Every day. Some even make it in winter. Can't get tired of it, they say. In fact, many Sicilians even have a special machine for this into which they toss ice, sugar and almonds and out comes an ice-white beauty. To get it to the same consistency as I ate it with the Sicilians, you will need an ice-cream machine to whip subtlety and life into it. Serve for breakfast with Pan brioche (opposite).

Put the almonds in a dry frying pan and toast gently until they just start to colour, turning them almost continuously. Watch that they don't darken, as this will change the milky white colour of the granita. Remove from the heat and cool completely.

Blend the almonds, sugar and roughly a cup of the water in a food processor until you have a smooth paste. Add the remaining water and blend to combine. Line a colander with muslin and set it over a deep bowl. Scrape the almond water into the colander and put aside, covered loosely, to drain overnight.

Remove the colander and, holding the almond–filled muslin over the bowl, twist and squeeze it firmly (taking care not to tear the fabric) to get the last of the milk from the pulp. You should have just under 750 ml (26 fl oz/ 3 cups) of almond milk. Now stir in 2 or 3 tablespoons of the almond pulp, depending on how much texture you like. You won't need the remaining pulp so you can discard it. Pour the milk into an ice-cream machine and churn following the manufacturer's instructions.

Once frozen store in a suitable container in the freezer and take it out a little before serving so it makes nice soft dollops in a cup, not hard scoops.

THE
LIST

12 g (¼ oz) FRESH YEAST

3 TABLESPOONS
TEPID MILK

2 EGG YOLKS, PLUS 1 EXTRA,
FOR BRUSHING

500 g (1 lb 2 oz/3⅓ cups) PLAIN
(ALL-PURPOSE) FLOUR

80 g (2¾ oz) BUTTER, MELTED

100 g (3½ oz) SUGAR

1 TEASPOON
VANILLA EXTRACT

1 TEASPOON ORANGE
FLOWER WATER

Makes 9

PAN BRIOCHE

The beauty of these rolls is in their lightness. My Sicilian friend insists they must be served with almond granita. They need to be made the night before, then left to rise, punched down, left to rise for a further 4 hours, shaped and left to rise once more before baking.

In a large bowl, crumble the yeast into the milk and leave for a few minutes, until bubbly. Add the 2 egg yolks and the rest of the ingredients, along with a pinch of salt. Mix to a soft dough, adding a little more flour or tepid milk as necessary. Knead on a lightly floured work surface until smooth and springy, about 5 minutes. Return to the bowl, cover with plastic wrap and then a cloth and leave in a warm spot to rise overnight.

Next morning, punch the dough down. Cover again and leave to rise in a warm place for about 4 hours, after which the dough will be very light and puffy. Line 2 baking trays with baking paper — they need to be trays with sides so you can put a cloth over the rising dough without it touching the dough. Punch the dough down again. Form into 9 oval-shaped rolls. Lay them on the trays now, as you won't be able to move them after they have risen. Leave, covered, until well puffed up.

Meanwhile, preheat the oven to 180°C (350°F/Gas 4). Whip the extra egg yolk and gently brush over the tops of the brioche with a pastry brush. Take care as they can easily deflate if you prod them too roughly. Bake for about 15 minutes, until pale gold. Remove to a wire rack to cool. Break off large pieces and scoop into Granita di mandorle (opposite). On their own they are great with butter and jam, plain or toasted.

COFFEE & CASSIA ICE CREAM

THE LIST

500 ml (17 fl oz/2 cups)
POURING (WHIPPING) CREAM

1 STICK OF CASSIA

1 TEASPOON
VANILLA EXTRACT

1 TEASPOON UNSWEETENED
COCOA POWDER

4 EGGS

120 g (4¼ oz) SUGAR

250 ml (9 fl oz/1 cup)
STRONG ESPRESSO COFFEE

Serves 8–10

I like to serve this with Brutti ma buoni (page 268) or sometimes with a blob of whipped cream on top. I use a 'moka' coffee maker to make a strong coffee.

Heat the cream, cassia stick, vanilla and cocoa powder in a large saucepan. Using electric beaters, whisk the eggs and sugar in a bowl until thick and pale.

When the cream is just coming to a boil stir in the coffee. Whisking constantly so nothing scrambles, slowly pour the cream and coffee mixture into the sugary eggs. Scrape it all back into the pan and return to a very low heat, whisking with a hand whisk to thicken slightly and cook the eggs. Take care not to scramble them.

When it is ready (it should coat the back of a spoon), remove from the heat and whisk regularly until it cools completely. Remove the cassia. Pour into an ice-cream machine and churn following the manufacturer's instructions. Alternatively, pour into a shallow tray and put in the freezer. When it is just frozen, after about 1 hour, beat vigorously with a fork to break up the ice crystals and then return the tray to the freezer. Repeat this process twice before leaving the ice cream to freeze completely. Store in the freezer in a sealed container.

GIANDUIA
ICE CREAM MATTONE
WITH WHIPPED CREAM

THE LIST

100 g (3½ oz) HAZELNUTS, SKINNED

500 ml (17 fl oz/2 cups) MILK

240 g (8½ oz) DARK UNSWEETENED CHOCOLATE, CHOPPED

4 TABLESPOONS DARK UNSWEETENED COCOA POWDER

4 WHOLE EGGS

150 g (5½ oz) SUGAR

1 TEASPOON VANILLA EXTRACT

250 ml (9 fl oz/1 cup) POURING (WHIPPING) CREAM

UNSWEETENED WHIPPED CREAM, TO SERVE

Serves 6–8

This is a chocolatey brick of ice cream topped with a pile of whipped cream. Quite delicious!

Line a 24 x 8 cm (9½ x 3¼ inch) loaf tin with plastic wrap or baking paper, leaving some overhang to make it easier to remove the ice cream. Toast 40 g (1½ oz) of the hazelnuts lightly in a dry frying pan, then chop them by hand to small bits. Put aside. Heat the milk in a large saucepan, then add the chocolate, stirring every now and then. When melted, stir in the cocoa and beat until smooth. Remove from the heat.

In a medium bowl, whisk the eggs with the sugar, vanilla and a pinch of salt until pale and creamy. Slowly dribble in some hot chocolate mixture, whisking so it doesn't scramble. When all the chocolate is incorporated pour the mixture back into the pan, add the chopped hazelnuts to infuse and put over very low heat. Whisking all the time, heat for a couple of minutes to cook out the eggs. There's no need to thicken. Remove from the heat and cool, whisking now and then.

Whisk in the cream, then cool in the fridge until well chilled. Strain the mixture directly into the prepared tin, and discard the hazelnuts. Put in the freezer to set.

Halve some of the remaining hazelnuts and quarter the rest. Toast them all in a dry frying pan with a light sprinkling of salt, then leave to cool. To serve the ice cream, unmould and cut into chunky slices. Serve one or two slices with dollops of whipped cream and some toasted hazelnuts scattered on top.

Altro che ringra...
tuj una quella
tque..... tratta....
tro che ringrati...
es.!

SAPIENTE
WORDS/PAROLE

MEASURE TWICE,
CUT ONCE

MILK & MINT
ICE CREAM

500 ml (17 fl oz/2 cups) MILK

100 g (3½ oz) SUGAR

ABOUT 16 MINT LEAVES

250 ml (9 fl oz/1 cup) POURING
(WHIPPING) CREAM

Serves 6–8

*This ice cream is delicate and subtle, and very easy to eat.
It's nice with a small biscuit, a square of dark chocolate
or just on its own.*

Heat the milk and sugar in a saucepan. Just as the milk is
coming to the boil, toss in the mint and then remove from
the heat. Leave it to infuse and cool down completely.

Remove the mint leaves with a slotted spoon and whisk
in the cream. Pour into an ice-cream machine and churn
following the manufacturer's instructions. Alternatively,
pour into a shallow tray and put in the freezer. When it is
just frozen, after about 1 hour, beat vigorously with a fork
to break up the ice crystals and then return the tray to
the freezer. Repeat this process twice before leaving the
ice cream to freeze completely. Store in the freezer in
a sealed container.

SAPIENTE
WORDS/PAROLE

TO LOOK AFTER YOUR BRUSHES,
WASH THEM IN MILK, THEN
RINSE IN WARM WATER AND LET
THEM DRY IN THE SUN

THE

LIST

LIMONCELLO SORBET

250 ml (9 fl oz/1 cup) WATER

1 LONG STRIP OF
LEMON RIND,
YELLOW PART ONLY

180 g (6¼ oz) SUGAR

JUICE OF 3 LEMONS
(ABOUT 150 ml/5 fl oz)

3 TABLESPOONS
BOUGHT OR HOME-MADE
LIMONCELLO (PAGE 17)

Makes just over 2 cups

Serve this with Fior di latte ice cream (opposite).
I love the combination of lemon and fior di latte.

Put the water, lemon rind and sugar in a pot. Bring to
the boil, then reduce the heat and simmer for 5 minutes.
Remove from the heat. Stir in the lemon juice and
the limoncello. Cool completely. Remove the strip of
lemon rind. Churn in an ice-cream machine following
the manufacturer's instructions. Store in the freezer
in a sealed container.

FIOR DI LATTE ICE CREAM

250 ml (9 fl oz/1 cup) MILK

A FEW DROPS OF
VANILLA EXTRACT

100 g (3½ oz) SUGAR

250 ml (9 fl oz/1 cup) POURING
(WHIPPING) CREAM

Makes just over 2 cups

Fior di latte is probably my favourite flavour in ice cream. Just milky cream. It always takes its partner to its best potential, and even alone is like a breath of fresh air.

Heat the milk in a pot with the vanilla and sugar, stirring until the sugar has dissolved. Remove from the heat and stir in the cream. Leave to cool completely. Churn in an ice-cream machine following the manufacturer's instructions. Alternatively, pour into a shallow tray and put in the freezer. When it is just frozen, after about 1 hour, beat vigorously with a fork to break up the ice crystals and then return the tray to the freezer. Repeat this process twice before leaving the ice cream to freeze completely. Store in the freezer in a sealed container.

SAPIENTE

WORDS/PAROLE

MY MOTHER ALWAYS SAID: NEVER RUN
AFTER A MAN OR A BUS — THERE IS
ALWAYS ANOTHER ONE COMING

Glossary

AGRETTI, also known as roscano or saltwort, is a grass-like spring vegetable from northern Italy that can often been found growing wild by salty marshes. It has a crisp, grassy freshness and is slightly tart and a bit salty.

ACACIA is a legume with pods and is edible, unlike its cousin mimosa. The acacias found in Europe are a different species to the thorny acacias of Australia and Africa.

BAIN MARIE is a water bath used to gently heat ingredients. In this book it is used to melt chocolate, by putting the chocolate in a heatproof bowl over a saucepan of simmering water. The base of the bowl must not come in contact with the water in order for the chocolate to melt without immediately setting again.

BURRATA is a rich, fresh, cow's milk cheese, similar in taste and appearance to a very creamy fresh mozzarella.

BUTTER used in Tuscany is most commonly unsalted. If you use salted butter to make these recipes be mindful of this when seasoning them.

CARDOONS, known as cardi in Italian, are a member of the thistle family. The stalks are eaten either raw when young or blanched, braised or baked when older and tougher.

CAVOLO NERO, literally meaning 'black cabbage', has loose, very dark-green leaves with stalks.

CHICKENS are often sold with their heads and legs attached from Italian butchers.

FLOUR in Italy is graded according to its gluten content or 'hard' qualities. The most commonly available are 0 (strong/bread flour) and 00, which is used for cakes and patisserie. However, there's a lot of contention about which type is best for what. I prefer hard flour for breads.

GUM ARABIC is sometimes known as acacia gum or Senegal gum. It is edible in small amounts and is tasteless, odourless and water-soluble so it makes a good adhesive for culinary uses, such as attaching decorations to cakes or biscuits.

HIMALAYAN SALT has pink and clear crystals, and comes from salt mines in Pakistan. It contains no preservatives or additives and is high in natural minerals.

INSALATA DI CAMPO/MISTICANZA translates literally as 'salad from the field' and is generally a mixture of fairly bitter leaves, such as various radicchio, endive, tops of wild fennel and flower tops, that varies with the seasons.

LARDO used in Tuscany is lardo di Colonnata, which originated around the Carrara marble mines. Cured with herbs (mainly rosemary) and spices, it is a pure white, soft rendered pork fat with a sweet smooth flavour. It is often used for wrapping foods before cooking, and thinly sliced pancetta can be substituted. It is also enjoyed on grilled or plain bread.

LAVENDER that is used for culinary purposes needs to be the edible variety, *lavandula augustafolia*, which is also known as true lavender, English lavender and lavender vera. Other varieties are not palatable and give an unpleasant soapy taste to foods.

MANITOBA FLOUR is obtained by milling varieties of hard wheat grown in North America, originally Manitoba in Canada. It forms a very high quantity of gluten during the kneading and cooking of bread.

MOKA COFFEE MAKER is the stove-top caffetiera loved by all Italians, who will have several machines of different sizes lined up on their kitchen shelf.

MURCOTT MANDARIN is a cultivar of tangerine that is sometimes called honey or honey murcott. It has a thin rind and strong flavour, and is very juicy. It can also have a lot of seeds.

PORCINI MUSHROOMS are also known as cepes or boletus, and are available from late summer into autumn in cooler regions. The thick white stem holds much of the flavour. When using fresh porcini, the stems need to be cooked for longer than the fleshy caps.

RED BULB SPRING ONIONS are bulb spring onions (scallions) with elongated, deep purple-red bodies and a mild sweet flavour.

RENNET APPLES are an old French variety, also called reinette, with firm, dry flesh, a strong flavour and long keeping, all of which make them ideal for cooking.

SALSICCIA is sausage, and can mean either fresh sausage, as in pork sausages, or cured, such as salamis. In this book, the salsiccia used is always fresh.

CHILLIES in Italy generally come from the sunny Italian south and are quite mild in flavour.

STRACCHINO is a rindless fresh cow's milk cheese that has a mild fresh taste.

VALERIANA is wild lamb's lettuce, also known as corn salad and mache. Watercress that has been picked over could be substituted.

ZIBBIBO RAISINS are small seedless dark raisins from the muscat grape.

Preserving and sterilising

PRESERVING

Whenever you are preserving foods, the ingredients should be as fresh as possible. Pack the fruit or vegetables into jars, seal with the lids and then process (bring to the boil and boil for at least 20 minutes) in the sealed jars. If the ingredients are not to be processed, any air bubbles should be removed by pushing the ingredients down with a fork. They should then always remain covered with their preserving liquid (oil, vinegar, syrup and so on).

When making jam, I have learned from my mother-in-law to spoon the hot jam into the clean sterilised jars, close the lids tightly and turn the jars upside down. They are left there, covered with a tea towel to cool completely. This creates a vacuum that can be seen on the lid, ensuring no air remains in the jars. The jars can then be stored upright in a cool, dark place for a few months. While it is safer to boil the jars, this is a quick and effective method. However, the time they will last depends on the amount of sugar you have used as it acts as preserving agent, so take special care when little sugar is used.

Use small, rather than large, jars for preserves as they can be used up quickly once opened. The tops or lids used should always be new and fit tightly. The jars should be kept in a cool, dark place until they are opened. After this, store them in the refrigerator and consume quickly. Clean cutlery should always be used when extracting the contents of the jars.

Home-made preserves that are not preserved in vinegar or salt and have no preservatives are more susceptible to bacteria as they lack the acidity that blocks their development. Take extra care with preserved foods to avoid botulism, a type of food poisoning caused by toxins from *Clostridium botulinum* bacteria. The bacteria can be present in tiny quantities and is very hard to detect, so if the contents of a jar ever look or smell suspicious, you should discard it.

STERILISING

To sterilise glass jars, wash them thoroughly in hot soapy water and then rinse under hot water. Place on a baking tray and put in an oven preheated to 120°C (235°F/Gas ½) until the jars are completely dry. Leave them in the oven until you are ready to fill them.

The
INDEX

A

acacia blossoms, fried 79
agretti 202
anchovies
    baked crumbed chicken with
      mozzarella, anchovies & capers 171
    crostini with anchovy, semi-dried
      tomato & mascarpone 80
    small round chillies stuffed with
      tuna & anchovy 27
    vegetables with 'bagna cauda' 99
apples
    Filomena's apple cake 272
    Leontine's apple cake 269
    pork shin with apples 219
    radicchio & apple salad 100
arista with rosemary & sage salt 220
artichokes
    artichoke & mint soup 92
    artichoke salad 202
    rosemary crumbed lamb chops,
      agretti & artichoke salad 201
    sautéed artichokes & potatoes 107
asparagus
    Barbara's asparagus & ham
      lasagne 128
    ravioli with asparagus, ricotta,
      sage & brown butter 126-7
autumn vegetable soup 96
avocado, spaghetti aglio, olio,
    peperoncino & 142

B

baci di dama 299
baci di Siena 307
Barbara's asparagus & ham lasagne 128
Barbara's Mum's spinach polpettine 152
basil liqueur 18
beef
    fillet with rose salt 197
    il bollito 209
    il lesso rifatto with onions 210
    meatballs from il bollito with potato 207
    meatballs in tomato 206
    pasta al forno Siciliana 131
    polpettone with onions 213
    ragu with milk & green tagliatelle 139
    scaloppine with tomatoes & capers 216
    stuffed guinea fowl 188
    stuffed onions 215
berries

fast focaccia with strawberries 53
mascarpone & lavender ice cream
    with wild strawberries 308
Nonna's blackberries al naturale 41
raspberry caramel pastries with
    crème fraîche 267-8
biscuits 270
    baci di dama 299
    lavender biscuits 283
    lemon biscuits with violets 282
    rose biscuits 281
bottles, removing deposits from 38
bread
    chicken ciabatta with valeriana,
      pecorino & hazelnut salad 181
    ciabatta (soul dough) 50
    crostini with anchovy, semi-dried
      tomato & mascarpone 80
    Emily's bread 55
    fast focaccia with strawberries 53
    filetto in crosta 227
    Marisa's pumpkin crostone 81
    pan brioche 313
    pan di rosmarino 66
    pancetta di Marisa 224
    stuffed guinea fowl 188
    tomato, mozzarella & herb
      bruschetta 85
breadcrumbed grilled calamari with
    Tabasco & thyme mayonnaise 251
brush care 322
brutta ma buoni 268

C

cakes
    Filomena's apple cake 272
    Granny Joy's marmalade cake 294
    Leontine's apple cake 269
    Nonna's dolce di Marie 295
    Nonna's egg white cake 289
    radicchio cake with white
      chocolate icing 275
    torta campagnola 290
    torta mimosa 290-1
    torta tartufata 276
cantuccini 289
capsicum
    chicken with peppers 164
    chilli & red pepper jam 37
cardoons, sautéed with parmesan 114
celery marmalade 34
chicken
    baked crumbed chicken with
      mozzarella, anchovies & capers 171
    chicken breast pie with porcini
      & sage 173
    chicken ciabatta with valeriana,
      pecorino & hazelnut salad 181
    chicken with peppers 164
    chicken with salsiccia & fennel 176
    collo ripieno 183
    grilled galletti 178
    Marisa's roast chicken 168
    roast lemon & thyme chicken 186
chickpeas with prawns 235
chilli
    chilli & red pepper jam 37
    small round chillies stuffed with

    tuna & anchovy 27
chocolate
    baci di Siena 307
    chocolate spread 276
ciabatta (soul dough) 50
coffee & cassia ice cream 314
collo ripieno 183
crostata di crema 284
crostata with peach jam 287
crostini with anchovy, semi-dried
    tomato & mascarpone 80

D

donzelle 62

E

eggs
    new garlic omelette 76
    omelette with blossoms 79
    torta di spaghetti 150
    vegetables with 'bagna cauda' 99
Emily's bread 55

F

fennel
    chicken with salsiccia & fennel 176
    Marta's Mum's fennel 103
    roast lamb & potatoes with wild fennel
      & semi-dried tomatoes 203
    sea bream with fennel & potatoes 236
filetto in crosta 227
fillet with rose salt 197
Filomena's apple cake 272
fior di latte ice cream 323
fish
    fish in a bottle 254
    fish with escarole, olives & capers 244
    persico with lemon, capers &
      green olive mash 239
    salmon trout with tarragon
      salsa verde 257
    scorfano with zucchini, cherry
      tomatoes & olives 250
    sea bream with fennel &
      potatoes 236
    small round chillies stuffed with
      tuna & anchovy 27
focaccia, fast, with strawberries 53
fruit salad tart 270

G

galletti, grilled 178
gilded frames, cleaning 102
Giovanna's spaghetti 145
granita di mandorle 312
Granny Joy's marmalade cake 294
grapes, roast rabbit with 187
green salad 102
green tagliatelle 140
guinea fowl, stuffed 188

H

ham
    Barbara's asparagus & ham
      lasagne 128
    ham & green olive tart 65
herbed oils 20
herbed vinegars 20

hiccups 164

I

ice cream
    coffee & cassia 314
    fior di latte 323
    gianduia ice cream mattone with
      whipped cream 317
    mascarpone & lavender ice cream
      with wild strawberries 308
    milk & mint 321
il bollito 209
il lesso rifatto with onions 210

J

jam
    chilli & red pepper 37
    peach 39
    quince 41
jars, sterilising 330
jasmine garlands 7
jelly, quince 40

L

la pizza fritta 57
lamb
    lamb with prunes and rosemary
      & sage salt 198
    roast lamb & potatoes with wild
      fennel & semi-dried tomatoes 203
    rosemary crumbed lamb chops,
      agretti & artichoke salad 201
lardo, prawns with lardo & insalata di
    campo 240
lavender biscuits 283
lavender sugar 42
lemon
    lemon biscuits with violets 282
    lemon pie 296
    Mariella's zucchini 115
    persico with lemon, capers
      & green olive mash 239
    risotto with prawns, lavender
      & lemon 155
    roast lemon & thyme chicken 186
lemon verbena peaches & cream 279
lemon verbena sugar 42
lentil ragu with spaghetti 134
Leontine's apple cake 269
lettuce, and carpets 224
limoncello 322
limoncello sorbet 322
linen cupboard 3
linen water 7

M

Mariella's zucchini 115
Marisa's potatoes with crumbs 106
Marisa's pumpkin crostone 81
Marisa's roast chicken 168
marmalade
    celery 34
    orange 38
    red radicchio 28
Marta's Mum's fennel 103
mascarpone & lavender ice cream
    with wild strawberries 308
mascarpone cream 279

mayonnaise, Tabasco & thyme 252
meat
    collo ripieno 183
    ragu with milk & green tagliatelle 139
meat, see also beef; lamb; pork
meatballs from il bollito with potato 207
meatballs in tomato 206
milk & mint ice cream 321
mozzarella
    baked crumbed chicken with
      mozzarella, anchovies & capers 171
    tomato, mozzarella & herb
      bruschetta 85

N

new garlic omelette 76
Nonna's blackberries al naturale 41
Nonna's dolce di Marie 295
Nonna's egg white cake 289
Nonna's plum & cognac mostarda 29

O

oils, herbed 20
olives
    fish with escarole, olives & capers 244
    Giovanna's spaghetti 145
    ham & green olive tart 65
    il lesso rifatto with onions 210
    persico with lemon, capers
      & green olive mash 239
    scorfano with zucchini, cherry
      tomatoes & olives 250
omelette with blossoms 79
onions
    il lesso rifatto with onions 210
    polpettone with onions 213
    stuffed onions 215
orange marmalade 38

P

pan brioche 313
pan di rosmarino 66
pancetta
    filetto in crosta 227
    rabbit, pancetta & rosemary pâté 167
    spaghetti with pancetta, pecorino
      & rosemary crumbs 141
pasta 120
    Barbara's asparagus & ham
      lasagne 128
    Giovanna's spaghetti 145
    green tagliatelle 140
    pasta al forno Siciliana 131
    penne with calamari, zucchini
      & flowers 133
    potato & truffle purses 122
    ragu with milk & green tagliatelle 139
    ravioli with asparagus, ricotta,
      sage & brown butter 126–7
    spaghetti aglio, olio, peperoncino
      & avocado 142
    spaghetti with clams, tomato
      & a dash of cream 146
    spaghetti with clams & Tabasco 149
    spaghetti with lentil ragu 134
    spaghetti with pancetta, pecorino
      & rosemary crumbs 141
    torta di spaghetti 150

peach jam 39
pears, risotto & pecorino with 156
penne with calamari, zucchini
    & flowers 133
pepper prawns 243
pepper salt 25
peppercorns, to repel insects 243
perfumed sugars 42
persico with lemon, capers & green
    olive mash 239
pizzas
    la pizza fritta 57
    pizza margherita 56
    sweet pizza 61
plum & cognac mostarda, Nonna's 29
Polish puff pastry 51
polpettone with onions 213
pork
    arista with rosemary & sage salt 220
    filetto in crosta 227
    pancetta di Marisa 224
    pork shin with apples 219
    stovetop pork in balsamic vinegar 223
potatoes
    Marisa's potatoes with crumbs 106
    meatballs from il bollito with
      potato 207
    persico with lemon, capers
      & green olive mash 239
    potato & truffle purses 122–3
    salt & balsamic vinegar sautéed
      potatoes 111
    salt & pepper potatoes with
      a trickle of buttermilk 110
    sautéed artichokes & potatoes 107
prawns with lardo & insalata di campo 240
preserved vegetables 14
preserving 330
puff pastry, Polish 51
pumpkin crostone, Marisa's 81

Q

quince jelly 40

R

rabbit
    rabbit, pancetta & rosemary pâté 167
    roast rabbit with grapes 187
radicchio
    radicchio & apple salad 100
    radicchio cake with white
      chocolate icing 275
    red radicchio marmalade 28
ragu with milk & green tagliatelle 139
raspberry caramel pastries with
    crème fraîche 267–8
ravioli with asparagus, ricotta, sage
    & brown butter 126–7
red radicchio marmalade 28
risotto with pears & pecorino 156
risotto with prawns, lavender
    & lemon 155
rose biscuits 281
rose salt 24
rose sugar 42
rosebuds, drying 282
rosemary & sage salt 24

rosemary crumbed lamb chops,
    agretti & artichoke salad 201

S

salads
    artichoke 202
    green salad 102
    radicchio & apple 100
    valeriana, pecorino & hazelnut 181
    valeriana salad 186
salmon trout with tarragon salsa
    verde 257
salsa verde 18
salt & balsamic vinegar sautéed
    potatoes 111
salt & pepper potatoes with a trickle
    of buttermilk 110
salts
    pepper 25
    rose 24
    rosemary & sage 24
    vanilla 25
sausage
    chicken with salsiccia & fennel 176
    collo ripieno 183
    stuffed guinea fowl 188
scallops, grilled, with truffle butter 259
scaloppine with tomatoes & capers 216
scorfano with zucchini, cherry
    tomatoes & olives 250
sea bream with fennel & potatoes 236
seafood
    breadcrumbed grilled calamari
        with Tabasco & thyme
        mayonnaise 251
    chickpeas with prawns 235
    grilled scallops with truffle butter 259
    grilled seppie & zucchini 75
    penne with calamari, zucchini
        & flowers 133
    pepper prawns 243
    prawns with lardo & insalata di
        campo 240
    risotto with prawns, lavender
        & lemon 155
    spaghetti with clams, tomato
        & a dash of cream 146
    spaghetti with clams & Tabasco 149
seafood, see also fish
soul dough 50
soup
    artichoke & mint 92
    autumn vegetable 96
    quick vegetable broth 156
    stracciatella 209
    tomato soup with rice & basil 95
spaghetti aglio, olio, peperoncino
    & avocado 142
spaghetti with clams, tomato
    & a dash of cream 146
spaghetti with clams & Tabasco 149
spaghetti with lentil ragu 134
spaghetti with pancetta, pecorino

    & rosemary crumbs 141
spinach
    Barbara's Mum's spinach
        polpettine 152
    green tagliatelle 140
stovetop pork in balsamic vinegar 223
stracciatella 209
sugars
    lavender 42
    lemon verbena 42
    rose 42
sweet pizza 61

T

Tabasco & thyme mayonnaise 252
tomatoes
    Barbara's Mum's spinach
        polpettine 152
    crostini with anchovy, semi-dried
        tomato & mascarpone 80
    meatballs in tomato 206
    roast lamb & potatoes with wild
        fennel & semi-dried tomatoes 203
    scaloppine with tomatoes & capers 216
    scorfano with zucchini, cherry
        tomatoes & olives 250
    spaghetti with clams, tomato
        & a dash of cream 146
    stuffed onions 215
    tomato, mozzarella & herb
        bruschetta 85
    tomato sauce 103
    tomato soup with rice & basil 95
    zucchini & flowers 115
torta campagnola 290
torta di spaghetti 150
torta mimosa 290-1
torta tartufata 276
truffles
    grilled scallops with truffle butter 259
    potato & truffle purses 122-3
    truffle butter 19

V

valeriana, pecorino & hazelnut salad 181
valeriana salad 186
vanilla salt 25
vegetables
    autumn vegetable soup 96
    preserved vegetables 14
    quick vegetable broth 156
    vegetables with 'bagna cauda' 99
vinegars, herbed 20
violets, drying 282

Z

zucchini
    grilled seppie & zucchini 75
    Mariella's zucchini 115
    penne with calamari, zucchini
        & flowers 133
    zucchini & flowers 115

Acknowledgements

Thank you to my team: photographer Manos, stylist Michail and
art director Lisa for your talent, endless creativity and inspiration.
To my sister-in-law Luisa and to Jo, my food editor, thanks for
your incredible help and support.
Thank you to Riccardo Barthel, for your generosity in letting
us in to your beautiful space (my FAVOURITE shop in Florence).
Thank you to David for creating the possibility, and Caterina
for the beautiful fabrics.

Thank you, Lisa McG, for your valuable support always.
To Mom, Ludi, Dad, Nin, Artemis, Leontine, Anabelle, Anjalika,
Barbara, Diana, Ketty, Julietta, Giovanna, Lucia, Laura, Matteo,
Ioanna, Joanna, Sylvia, Luisa, Paolo, Cetina, Lidia, Mariella, Marzia,
Olga, Marisa, Marta, Filomena, Pierluigi, Emily, Peta, Patrizia,
Rebecca, Jan, Carmella, Claudia, Nicci, Roberto, Filippo, Massimo,
Gianluca, Carlos, Trong, Jackie - thank you all for your recipes
and the many other gracious ways you have helped.
Thank you to all at Murdoch. To my publishers, Sally and Chris -
thank you for your trust. And to my editor Anna, to Livia, Deborah
and the many others involved in making this book - thank you for
your hard work.
Thank you, Giovanni, Yasmine and Cassia, my precious family -
for your patience, your encouragement.
To Mario - thank you for sharing your knowledge and for all
these beautiful photographs you took of Wilma.
And finalmente, Wilma - thank you for all you have given.

x Tessa

Published in 2012 by Murdoch Books Pty Limited

Murdoch Books Australia
Pier 8/9
23 Hickson Road
Millers Point NSW 2000
Phone: +61 (0) 2 8220 2000
Fax: +61 (0) 2 8220 2558
www.murdochbooks.com.au
info@murdochbooks.com.au

Murdoch Books UK Limited
Erico House, 6th Floor
93–99 Upper Richmond Road
Putney, London SW15 2TG
Phone: +44 (0) 20 8785 5995
Fax: +44 (0) 20 8785 5985
www.murdochbooks.co.uk
info@murdochbooks.co.uk

For Corporate Orders & Custom Publishing contact Noel Hammond,
National Business Development Manager Murdoch Books Australia

Publisher: Sally Webb
Design concept: Lisa Greenberg
Design coordination: Robert Polmear
Photographer: Manos Chatzikonstantis
Stylist: Michail Touros
Food Editor: Jo Glynn
Editor: Anna Scobie
Project Manager: Livia Caiazzo
Production Manager: Karen Small

A cataloguing-in-publication entry is available from the catalogue of
the National Library of Australia at www.nla.gov.au.

A catalogue record for this book is available from the British Library.

Printed by 1010 Printing International Limited, China

We would like to thank Riccardo Barthel in Florence for lending items for use and
photography.

IMPORTANT: Those who might be at risk from the effects of salmonella poisoning (the
elderly, pregnant women, young children and those suffering from immune deficiency
diseases) should consult their doctor with any concerns about eating raw eggs.

OVEN GUIDE: You may find cooking times vary depending on the oven you are using.
For fan-forced ovens, as a general rule, set the oven temperature to 20°C (35°F) lower
than indicated in the recipe.

We have used 20 ml (4 teaspoon) tablespoon measures. If you are using
a 15 ml (3 teaspoon) tablespoon add an extra teaspoon of the ingredient
for each tablespoon specified.

0203687002 9

020 3156 8 954